Oswald John Simon

Faith and Experience

A Selection of Essays and Addresses

Oswald John Simon

Faith and Experience
A Selection of Essays and Addresses

ISBN/EAN: 9783337279912

Printed in Europe, USA, Canada, Australia, Japan

Cover: Foto ©Lupo / pixelio.de

More available books at **www.hansebooks.com**

FAITH AND EXPERIENCE.

FAITH AND EXPERIENCE.

A SELECTION OF

ESSAYS AND ADDRESSES

BY

OSWALD JOHN SIMON,

(LATE OF BALLIOL COLLEGE, OXFORD),

AUTHOR OF "THE WORLD AND THE CLOISTER," ETC., ETC.

LONDON:
WERTHEIMER, LEA & CO.,
CIRCUS PLACE, LONDON WALL.

1895.

DEDICATION.

IN EVER FOND MEMORY OF

THREE BROTHERS.

J. D. S., DIED 29TH MAY, 1873, AGED 26,

A. O. S., DIED 21ST OCTOBER, 1882, AGED 28,

W. G. S., DIED 6TH JULY, 1894, AGED 43.

"First of all there is the thought of rest and freedom from pain; they have gone home, as the common saying is, and the cares of this world touch them no more. Secondly, we may imagine them as they were at their best and brightest, humbly fulfilling their daily round of duties—selfless, childlike, unaffected by the world; when the eye was single and the whole body seemed to be full of light; when the mind was clear and saw into the purposes of God. Thirdly, we may think of them as possessed by a great love of God and man, working out His will at a further stage in the heavenly pilgrimage. And yet we acknowledge that these are the things which eye hath not seen nor ear heard, and therefore it hath not entered into the heart of man in any sensible manner to conceive them. Fourthly, there may have been some moments in our own lives when we have risen above ourselves, or been conscious of our truer selves, in which the will of God has superseded our wills, and we have entered into communion with Him, and been partakers for a brief season of the Divine truth and love, in which like Christ we have been inspired to utter the prayer, 'I in them, and thou in me, that we may be all made perfect in one.' These precious moments, if we have ever known them, are the nearest approach which we can make to the idea of immortality."

JOWETT.

CONTENTS.

		PAGE
1.	Divine and Human	1
2.	To be Alone	15
3.	Experience	27
4.	An Essay on Tact	39
5.	The Pulpit: its Defects, its Possibilities	53
6.	Missionary Judaism	69
	(From the "Jewish Quarterly Review.")	
7.	Reformed Judaism	90
	(From the "Jewish Quarterly Review.")	
8.	The Universal Element in Judaism	111
	(Published in Philadelphia, U.S.A.)	
9.	The Day of Memorial	126
	(From the "Jewish Chronicle.")	
10.	Denominational Schools	139
	(From the "Jewish Chronicle.")	
11.	Man's Relation to God	152
	(Sermon at Hackney Synagogue, 1886.)	
12.	The Mission of Israel	166
	(Discourse in Manchester, 1887.)	
13.	The Divine Presence	181
	(Discourse delivered at West Hampstead, April 26, 1870.)	
14.	Higher Judaism	195
	(Discourse delivered at Kilburn Town Hall, March 19, 1892.)	
15.	Religious Calm	206
	(A Sermon preached at the Reform Synagogue in Manchester, July 2, 1892.)	
16.	The Liberty of the Soul	216
	(Printed in 1885.)	
17.	Introspection	224
	(Printed in 1885.)	
18.	The Master of Balliol.—In Memoriam	238

FAITH AND EXPERIENCE.

DIVINE AND HUMAN.

MEN and women are capable of acquiring knowledge and of gathering experience in regard to the relation between what is Divine and what is human. There is, however, a common impression that in this world we can only learn about our humanity; there is not much, it is said, that we can attain in the knowledge of the Divine nature. This is the supposition among people of a certain order of mind. There are others who believe that there is a definite revelation of the Divine nature in the Scriptures, but that this revelation is to be found nowhere else. Such a view may be said to represent particular types of religionists—not uncommon—among Jews and Christians. The ordinary phrase, "to believe in God," does not convey all that is meant by a revelation of the Divine nature. What is human, what is Divine, are questions which can be answered in the pages of the Bible, but also in the record of general human experience. There is not, indeed, any sharp line drawn between the spheres of the Divine and human. The two join one another, and are only quite distinct at their extremities.

The doctrine of the union between the Divine and human is not new. It has indeed given rise to many assumptions in regard to the manifestation of the Divine nature in human form. To those who are not Christians, and to many who are, there is something unsatisfactory in the proposition that the union of these two natures was manifested only at a particular time and in one individual. The Divinity of Jesus, even to those who believe that he was the incarnation of the Deity, does not express all that I would venture to submit as to the representation of the union of God and man. To say that God once took upon Himself our nature, and that He ascended from the grave into heaven with our nature still upon Him, is but a partial and isolated instance of that union of which I speak. Whether historically true or untrue, the idea as an abstract conception does not carry with it very much more than the notion of a single supernatural transaction. The union of the human character with the Divine nature still would remain an open question. Even with the admission, which one cannot logically withhold, that a single instance of Divine embodiment under any circumstances whatever does postulate the idea of intimate relations between the Divine and the human, the relation in such a case as that is not the same as the more general and permanent assimilation in human character of the Divine element. Moreover, in the story of the Gospels the incarnation is not merely an individual instance of two natures in one person, but it is expressly conditioned by exceptional circumstances. And beyond this special limitation the whole episode is founded upon the hypothesis that there is not an inherent affinity between the two, but rather that such affinity had to be acquired by supernatural intervention. The order of things upon the Christian view of God's condescension is one which presupposes a gulf between the Divine and human, only capable of being bridged by a stupendous miracle.

Now what is proposed to be here considered is the general and permanent assimilation in human character of something which is Divine. Starting from the point of view which takes cognisance of human nature in all its frailty, subject to many temptations, some of which belong almost to the physical circumstance of human life, and recognising the fact of sin as one of the risks and dangers incidental to the human pilgrimage, is there yet within the forces of human character some power stronger and more subtle than any which is merely human? Is there at least a possibility that the higher culture of the moral faculties in man may rise to a height of development in which the will itself becomes invested with some attribute that might be regarded as the counterpart of a Divine quality? We all know that steadfast resistance of evil does in due course emancipate the human soul from the slavery of the grosser passions. Worldly temptations as well as the snares of the flesh, are things which do sometimes become actually plucked out from the roots of human susceptibility. It is an experience with some gifted natures, that certain evils which present terrific temptations to ordinary persons, have absolutely no power of attraction whatsoever. There is no more even the consciousness of a struggle, for the struggle is over and the moral victory complete. The desire to do and to think that which is incompatible with the highest moral culture ceases to invade itself upon the individual thus purified and elevated. Qualities such as jealousy, envy, and lust are removed at so great a distance that they stand in relation to a soul of this type in a like position in which obnoxious food would appear to a healthy digestion. The conquest of sin in its ordinary forms is not an occurrence so rare as to be counted a miracle. In addition to those cases of conquest after long and fierce inward encounter with temptation, there are other natures in which there was never any need for such encounter in regard to the lower temptations. Some persons are born with moral endowments which render them free from many of those temptations with which throughout life others are beset. Yet for all inequalities in the moral attributes of different men and women there is still a race to run even for those who are best endowed. In the finest natures, largely liberated from the trammels of palpable temptation and mortal sin, there are qualities which have to be acquired. It is certain that there are degrees higher and lower in which certain virtues may be cultivated. Beyond a certain point, within which we are in the habit of describing qualities as simply human, there are possibilities of development to higher points in the moral compass that may be said to be divine. A striking illustration is the virtue of charity. From the ordinary point of view, charity is a virtue with varying standards. That which satisfies the claims of society is somewhat bald, and does not rise beyond very simple human requirements. A person is said to be charitable if he is willing to devote some portion of his surplus means to the benefit of others. Giving alms is a common interpretation of charity. Giving service is just a little above it. But there are higher regions, such as forgiveness of injury, which may be said to partake of the Divine attribute of pardon. There are moreover particular attitudes of the intellect, induced and regulated by the spiritual faculties, which seem to bring the human will into a kind of co-operation with the purposes of God. There is the estimate which we form of our fellow mortal, which may approach in resemblance the view that we could suppose to be entertained by God himself. Intense commiseration for others, because of the temptations to which they are subject, and an inexhaustible pity on account of their sins is perhaps the nearest approach we can make to the likeness of God.

To estimate others by a standard different from that by which we measure our own actions, is a soaring upwards toward the Divine manner of thought. Hence it is that there is no more conspicuous instance of the Divine element in human character, than that which prompts men and women to rescue people from sin. In our own generation there has been a powerful development of this tendency manifested in the various works that are being accomplished in the rescue of fallen women, the creation of fresh opportunities for discharged convicts, and in the foundation of homes for homeless children. The attempt to cope with evils arising from sin or the hereditary consequences of sin is something which in a marked degree manifests the Divine nature in human character. "Inasmuch as ye do to the least of these, ye do unto me" is a principle which, one is thankful to recognise, is exercising considerable sway over the minds of many men and women. So too that thought in the Hebrew Scriptures, that the holiness of the Divine Being is a reason for the holiness of mankind, intertwines the Divine and human with wonderful force. How far ideas such as these have entered into the general conception of the moral life is a question which cannot easily be answered.

There is a popular notion that the moral attributes of God, and those of man are different in kind as well as in degree. True that some attributes of the Supreme Being must necessarily differ from those of humanity, but are they such as belong to the domain of morals? In the case of power and of will there are of course in the Divine personality the attributes of immensity and of eternity. God is infinite not only in the sense in which we speak of space. For in the case of space, indefiniteness is rather what is meant when we say it is infinite. Infinity in respect to the Almighty God on the other hand is not indefiniteness but a definite attribute. In relation to such matters as these, there is difference between the human and divine which cannot be measured by degrees. We are altogether, and of necessity, upon a distinct plane from that in which we are bound to conceive the Supreme Being. But when we come to the consideration of moral attributes,—love, charity, and goodwill, are we not dealing with ideas which are specially revealed to us as the manifestations of a Divine nature? In the case of some moral attributes which are distinctively human, such as obedience, resignation, and humility, we are again placed upon a different plane from that of our Divine Creator. These are attributes which cannot logically be applied to Him. They are essentially human virtues—qualities imposed upon the moral nature of our own species as things pertaining to us and to us alone. But they do not exhaust the category of qualities which are essential to the highest moral development of human character. Other virtues are indispensable, namely, charity, with compassion, patience, and forgiveness. These, on the other hand, do represent to us the counterparts at least of distinctive attributes of God himself. Now the power of love, when it is distinguished from that which is subject to the relations of sex, ceases to be merely a human quality. When it is of such a character that it is no longer dependent upon physical conditions, such as the love of kindred or of romance, it becomes transfigured, and may be regarded as the revelation of the Divine nature in human character. The ideal of Christ, which whether historical or fictional, carries the most profound impression upon our moral susceptibilities, consists first of his purity, then of the tenderness and the depth of his affections. The singular attractiveness which belongs to that personality is probably something which is missed in the ordinary view, namely, the profound capacity to love his species. Just as the Creator is represented as regarding human beings in the light of His own children and loving them with a parental love, so in this ideal we have the notion of intense fraternal love spreading its wing of unselfish devotion over the whole span of the human race. There is nothing in human experiences which so strikingly reveals the Divine nature as the aptitude on the part of some rare and gifted individuals to love a great many people. Love in the limited human sense is something which is scarcely comparable with the Divine attribute of love. When we contemplate the faculty of affection in the average man and woman, and then contemplate it as it is in the Supreme Being, we perceive two distinct conditions. The one is an image of the other, but so infinitesimal that they can scarcely be measured by degrees. On the other hand, human character is capable of so great a development under spiritual influence that it is possible to acquire a very much larger capacity of affection than that which is sufficient for one's family and one's friends. All human affection in its common types proceeds actually from the love of self. Whereas the higher love of which I speak is nothing but the expression of the love of God. We love our children or our parents and other blood relations because our personal well-being is bound up with theirs. Husband and wife, or persons of opposite sex who are contemplating marriage, love one another, too, because the personal happiness of the one is bound up with that of the other. It is not on this account an ignoble passion any more than in the other cases. The love of self is not a sin, because it is a natural instinct, and therefore a Divine decree. But the love to those who neither belong to us by kinship nor by personal friendship, and in whom none of our personal interests are bound, is a Divine love. It might be questioned whether the term is applicable to the case. It might be urged that some other word was needed to express any sentiment of good feeling which might be entertained in these circumstances. But we mean nothing less than love, we mean an unselfish sacrifice for their good, a caring for, a deep, pitying, long-suffering sympathy, which will prompt us to take pains to promote their welfare even at the risk of our own. Such was the ideal in the character of Christ. It was nothing less than that. The Divine attribute of love may too be manifested in the ordinary domestic relations. Even between those of close kinship there can be a difference between the commonplace or merely human affection, and something higher which is touched by the Divine impress. It does sometimes occur that very great unselfishness is required to give force to the true love between parents and children, brothers and sisters, and even other relations. One may so love the memory of the dead as to make great sacrifices in order to act towards some one who was dearest to them. This is a kind of guardianship which springs from the Divine attribute of love. In all human relationships there are the two ways of seeing things. There is self-interest on the one hand, on the other there is the possibility of viewing a matter as seen in the light of God. To see anything as He sees it is certainly an indication that human character may assimilate to itself something which is divine. What is commonly called disinterestedness is perhaps a mode of expressing that idea.

In the matter of judgment the Divine element

may enter into human speculation. What is called the worldly man is a type of character which does not partake of Divine qualities. He sees things differently. His judgment is tarnished by worldly considerations. He does not look with the eye of faith. He cannot imagine how things are estimated by the Divine judgment. Seeing with unerring eyes is not the gift of the worldly vision. On the other hand the spiritual insight of those who habitually live in the presence of God gives a force and a wisdom to their judgment which is altogether lacking in the ungodly. Some of us must have observed in some fine natures a keen penetration into the conditions of those with whose habit of life they are not so familiar as the worldly man. Yet they see more clearly and are possessed of a wonderful perception by no means common among ordinary people. This is the reason why it is better in difficult and controversial subjects to seek the advice of one whose life is spiritual than of one who lives only for the world. First of all it is a calmer judgment. Secondly, it is a judgment which is lifted above those influences which are likely to render it prejudiced and one-sided. The spiritual character has imagination about it. The mind of such a one "is stayed" on God, and is therefore possessed of an inward peace which the worldly one cannot experience. There is then a judicial impartiality; and a person of this description will not merely observe all the facts of the case, but will measure them by other standards than those which are suggested only by the limited experience of one's personal surroundings. He will look at motives, he will estimate temptations, and take into account many subtle and inward forces which generally escape the attention of the man of the world. In these ways we get a glimpse of the meaning of divine judgment. In other words we come into contact with the Divine element in human character. The story of the prodigal son is a remarkable instance of the application of a Divine judgment on the part of men. From the common point of view, not Divine, there would be no concern for the restoration of those who are spiritually lost. It is the Divine quality in human character, and that alone, which suggests the idea of joy in connection with reclaiming people from sin, and indeed which prompts efforts on their behalf.

The Divine element in human character is manifested again in a variety of ways which create and stir up sacred confidences between persons who might be supposed to have very little in common. There is a religious sympathy between two individuals who hold different views about religion. The explanation is probably that the Divine element in the character of both is so strong that it supersedes the human elements which form the source of their different opinions. Among persons with whom the Divine element is weak or uncultivated, all that is apparent between them is their difference of conviction. They cannot agree because they do not think alike upon the same subject. All that engages them is the sense of difference. The power of the Divine element in human character is so strong and so forcible that it entirely overlaps the merely human view of things. The moment we come into touch with the Divine nature we are filled with the sense of unity. The person who regards God as being known only to one particular Communion has failed to apprehend the nature of God. This is the reason why throughout history religion has invariably been represented as a badge of separation rather than as a bond of union. In other words, men have been preoccupied with their own views, which were only human, and have not let in to the mind the flood light which flows from the Divine source alone. In order to appropriate in our own characters something of the Divine nature we must give ourselves to a more purified worship of the Divine Being. We must yield what is merely human in order to gain something which is Divine. Hence it is that there is no prayer which is so blessed as the prayer that asks for nothing. The silent kneeling supplicant, alone in darkness, will be the first to receive Divine light. The secret of the love of God is its Divine element. It is unlike other kinds of love. Its confiding power is so great that it is unbaffled even by the mystery of suffering. The covenant between an individual soul and the Supreme Being whom it loves is of such a nature as to awaken wonder in the ordinary mind. Nothing shakes the faith when once that Divine love is established. It can face all things, it can bear all burdens. Perhaps the most striking instance within recent observation of such love between a man and his God was that of the late General Gordon. There are doubtless many more of whom the world knows nothing. The kind of devotion here manifested is something different from the usual attachment between one person and another. Human qualities without a spark of the Divine nature would be unequal to the enormous strains which humanly speaking that love requires. The sentence in the Book of Job, "Though he slay me yet will I trust in him," expresses this peculiar kind of love—a kind not to be found among ordinary mortals.

TO BE ALONE.

"In the multitude of my thoughts within me Thy comforts delight my soul."—*Psalm* xciv. 19.

THERE is a vast difference between being alone and being lonely. It is essential that we should sometimes be alone, but it is never desirable to be lonely. Again, we must carefully distinguish between being alone and eschewing intercourse with our fellow-men. The subtle and complex character of human nature requires for its proper development conditions which seem opposed to one another. Human intercourse is a vital condition in every life, but retirement into "the inner chamber" is also indispensable. There are times in every thoughtful life when isolation is quite as needful as society. And in saying this it is not forgotten that social intercourse has a value which is not always fully estimated. The mingling of acquaintances, quite apart from the association of intimate friends with the unspeakable happiness which it is able to afford, has a good in itself that may properly be regarded as constituting a distinct element in the building up of character. There is, too, an incipient mischief in the tendency of those who habitually prefer to be without companions. But here we propose to consider the special advantages of regular intervals of isolation, and to say what it is which constitutes both the need and the purpose of being thus alone.

This question has many bearings, but spiritually the boon of occasional seclusion is greater than some are apt to imagine. We do not here refer to the benefit of quiet so obviously demanded for ordinary purposes of work and duty. We are alluding to the spiritual aspect of human nature, that one whose very nourishment depends primarily upon rest, repose, and at times even introspection. I refer to introspection with some hesitation, because it is a subject which requires great care in contemplating it. A good deal that passes for introspection is very often nothing but the impetus to a dangerous self-consciousness. The retirement and isolation which is needful at times for every human soul admits, however, of different kinds of introspection. A tranquil conscience is, above all things, the one essential guarantee for that higher happiness to which even in this sphere of care and difficulty every mortal is entitled. The conditions for securing and preserving such tranquillity depend among other gifts upon the administration, so to speak, of a certain solitude. There are inward processes of purification to which periodical and systematic isolation is necessary. Some people are seldom or never really alone. They live in an unbroken atmosphere of confusion and social excitement;

they do not often allow themselves to commune with their own hearts and be still. There is an unceasing disquietude; or, in others again, that which is superficial seems to hold sway, and they rarely think or pray.

Prayer is a condition of human effort requiring, above all things, a well-ordered isolation. There is all the difference between that reflection which awakens prayer and another kind that sets one brooding. The element of ordinary loneliness, which distinguishes that state from the one which I have described as *being alone*, does not enter at all into the condition which we are here considering. The element of loneliness having about it sometimes gloom, too frequently an unhealthy self-consciousness, is absent in the higher condition of *being alone*, just because at such times we are not spiritually alone. One might almost describe the two kinds of loneliness thus. One brings merely the consciousness of self, the other the consciousness of God. And it is just this higher consciousness that completely alters the tones of human susceptibility when our isolation is the means of bringing us into contact with God rather than that of merely separating us from other mortals. This distinction is of the utmost consequence. There can be cultivated a certain habit of isolating oneself—not for the purpose of shunning our own species, but in order to draw ourselves consciously into the Divine presence. The Omnipresence of God is probably the most stupendous truth which religion has to teach. It is also a familiar phrase, so familiar, indeed, that it is apt to lose its weighty significance in relation to our personal affairs. God is everywhere, men say; but do we frequently take cognisance of His immediate presence? The nearness of God is not always easy to realise. Life is too full of such influences that seem to act upon us in a way to veil our inward vision of God, and take us far away from Him. It is not a common thing to live always as though God were actually with us. And yet a person who believed He was not there might consider himself an agnostic or an atheist. To be alone is one of the most helpful ways of finding ourselves with God, though it would be far from the truth to assert that the mere fact of shutting ourselves off from others was in itself sufficient to enable us to realise God; but by being alone in the sense which I would endeavour to make plain, very much more is implied than what is commonly understood by isolation.

To believe in God is not quite the same thing as to live with God. The difference is equal to the difference between the passive and the active moods. Companionship with a human friend is surely something unlike the condition in which we say we have a friend far away from us. The intimacies of frequent intercourse are scarcely possible, and certainly only rarely maintained, when the friend is constantly absent. When we speak of keeping friendship in repair, we mean that the long silence of distance and separation should be occasionally broken. It may be by a visit, or a letter, or only an inquiry. But imagine a permanent removal from an old friend with whom no sort of communication takes place for a number of years. That friendship may survive the strain in rare instances. It may linger in memory on one side or the other fortified at times by the recurrence of tender thoughts. But in the majority of cases do not the springs of friendship and of mutual interest dry up in such circumstances? We may, after a lapse of time, meet again the old familiar friend, and our affections are perhaps renewed. It happens with old schoolfellows or college friends whom we had once cared for, and in whose society we found happiness, that a long separation occurs through no particular fault on either side, and the chance meeting in later years revives everything in a moment. In ten minutes it may seem as though we had never been parted. So with a long absent brother with whom the sacred domestic tie had never actually been loosened; but then it is because, despite distance and changed circumstances, the two hearts remained faithful. Nothing had occurred during the interval to chill the one or to estrange the other. Likewise the memory of our beloved dead can be retained through a long survivorship, continuing, perhaps, from the vigour of manhood when the companion of our life, near in age, and close in intimacy, had been suddenly wrenched from the very foundations of that structure which composed our world, leaving a void that is never filled, until old age is upon us and the memory of the lost one is still sweet and precious and tender; or those we have lost in earlier life, a contemporary in the household, or even an older person who, in the course of nature, could not have run out with us the sand-glass of time, whom indeed, we must have survived if we ourselves had not died in youth. There, too, the image may remain ever bright and glowing. But in all these cases the sustaining power of our love is the secret of this preservation in remembrance of a devoted one long since gone. We have visited the grave, we have had their pictures about us. We have treasured their written words and other relics of a devoted past. Moreover, we have been conscious by our very union with God that we were still in union with them, He being the one eternal Father in whose keeping they repose. But in all this there has been an active principle at work, namely, the secret life. We have been alone, we have had interests apart from, and independent of those which belong only to the world and to society and to ordinary affairs. So, in like manner, the relation with God, as with human objects of affection whom we cannot grasp with the mortal hand, depends upon our being sometimes alone—not always within the gaze of a tumultuous world or conventional social surroundings.

The worship of God, which is indeed the highest privilege of human nature, is only truly conducted when there is a sense of no other presence but His own. The approach which we make to God, whether in our private room or at public worship, begins with the casting off all else. It may be on the sea-shore or in the midst of country life, but we must be alone. Even in a vast congregation the soul which finds God is that one which is alone, not hindered by the surrounding impressions of other people, or of discordant note, or an unsympathetic voice. It was God we went to seek. It was He only, whom we looked for in that place, and no other came between us. The very nature of prayer requires a certain secrecy as between the individual and Him who is approached. It is no prayer at all where the ordinary reserve, proper in other conditions, lies like a curtain over the heart, stinting the free expression of itself, and dictating words which have only a general and not a personal meaning. No published formula can at all times express exactly what a single soul has to say to God. The fact that it is the language of public worship often renders it unfitting for private use. This, however, is not always the case. There are prayers in every liturgy, and, above all, phrases in the Psalter, which to those who are familiar with them seem on some occasions to rise to the lips as the precise words that are needed if we would articulate the prayer which is within. In the matter of prayer the soul seeks to realise its individual relation with God. And for this purpose it must be alone with Him.

But apart from the office of prayer, there are other incidents of life, partly spiritual, partly intellectual, which demand that we must exercise our reflective powers in a way that would be hindered if we were in the presence of others. Prayer is the great instrument by which we preserve through life our conscious relations with the Deity, just as others that I have mentioned are the instruments by which we preserve our relations with those who are not visible to the mortal eye. but for whom we still entertain love and devotion. But in all busy lives there are perpetually arising problems which call for careful solution. It must be within the experience of many persons that there is a difference between the judgment we form of a question when we are surrounded by people and that which we decide upon when we are alone. In deliberative assembly it is likely to happen that some idea is sprung upon us which we had not previously thought about. It is not a safe plan in that case to determine at once the course we should take in regard to it. Probably the matter will be presented there and then from different points of view, and we may hear from various speakers much that can be said in favour of it and against it. We may be induced to form our own opinions about it and be willing to pronounce upon it ere we depart. And yet when we have left our colleagues and are alone, some fresh light may dawn upon us in respect to that particular question. We may wonder that we had not seen the subject in that light before. With some persons the tendency to think in different ways when they are alone, and when they are not alone, is greater than with others. But with all people there are matters affecting the springs of human conduct and of feeling which are far better considered away from other people. When you are on a visit you receive a letter about affairs which you would not mention to anybody in the house. You may read the letter in a room where there are people, but you will prefer to think the matter over by yourself. What a sense of relief there is when you find yourself in your private room or out of doors alone. Then again there are moods and conditions in ordinary human experience when the mere presence of a second person is a hindrance to the process of making up your mind about a certain duty. Our powers of judgment—rarely strong, often weak—are greatly marred when we are not by ourselves. One of the most subtle drawbacks in a defective eyesight is our dependence upon other people either for being read to or for writing at our dictation. Those who have never been thus afflicted cannot easily imagine the strain upon the mental and the spiritual faculties which were necessary before we could in any degree overcome the obstacle. To be alone with an author, and to be alone with your own pen, seem to be the natural requirements alike for the reader and for the writer. Some thoughts do not enter our minds if anybody is with us. There is a certain influence, not always consciously felt, when there is any other person near. A student will discover when he has left his study and enters the presence of other people a sense of amazement that but a few minutes ago his state of mind was so unlike what it is now. The whole nature would seem to be transformed. On the other hand it is desirable that we should not shut our eyes to the opposite side of this truth. The presence of some one individual near and dear to us may exercise a stimulating effect upon our work. It is conceivable that some eminent thinkers may have felt themselves under a powerful impetus when there was in their study the one person to whom they were most endeared The presence of a child does, with certain temperaments, carry with it a sweetening influence upon their thoughts and their work. But instances of this kind only tend to support the proposition that there is a special value in removing oneself at times from ordinary people, for those cases are rare indeed in which in moments of deep reflection any second presence can be of value.

One of the greatest facts in human life is the unfitness of man to be always alone. The need of companionship is obviously greater with some natures than with others; but there is no properly constituted human being who will be improved by having no companions. Isolation should be temporary rather than the permanent condition of life. In other words, it should never be regarded except as a means to an end. Human fellowship, above all things, is the main condition for which individuals ought to train themselves. And such intervals of separating ourselves are only good so far as they afford us the opportunity of rendering us more fit for the society of others. Undoubtedly a large part of the education in after life, the cultivation of the intellect, the purification of the spirit and the formation of convictions must be accomplished chiefly in solitude. Those who never permit themselves to be alone in this sense are apt to miss the kind of training here mentioned. But society in its fuller sense, that is, the communion of mind with mind and the quickening of human sympathy, are, after all, the essential characteristics of the earthly pilgrimage. Whether the surroundings be those of a domestic life, or whether the family relationship is restricted, whether we are married or unmarried, or indeed if even we are without kindred, intercourse with others must for ever be regarded as the purpose and not the mere accident of our being. Nor is it good in a state of domestic happiness to confine one's interest entirely to the family. For a centre, for hallowing influences, this is beyond doubt the truly ideal, but the capacity of the human intellect and of the emotions is wider than we are apt to think. A love of our species is the best expression we can make of the love of God. The greatest souls who have ever lived were those whose love spread far beyond the limits of the family and of the home. The late revered master of Balliol, Professor Jowett, wisely wrote that there may be indeed "some rare nature who will feel his duty to another generation, or to another century, almost as strongly as to his own."

EXPERIENCE.

EXPERIENCE and conviction act and react upon one another in a striking degree. Many of the convictions that constitute the opinions or the creed of an individual are the result of other forces than that of experience, or, at least, other than the force of personal experience. The experiences of history, seen under different aspects, will naturally be the basis, alleged or assumed, of a man's political doctrine, still more of the political doctrine of a party. In religion and philosophy, however, personal experience, as distinct from the experience of others, ought to be a much more potent influence in forming settled views. A mind which is given up to criticism, or in which the critical faculty has been developed to the neglect of other faculties, does not find it easy to form definite convictions. It has never allowed itself to experience anything beyond the doubts and uncertainties surrounding the propositions of different schools of thought. To have felt something to be true, that is, to have experienced it, is naturally a more weighty matter than to have been induced to believe it by the evidences of others. It is admitted that there is a large domain of human thought and feeling which lies outside the sphere of mathematical demonstration. To what extent religion and philosophy are found to travel in that outer region no one would pretend to say. True it is that within the limits of demonstration there resides much that may lead us to determine how and in what manner we shall think. But as to what we shall believe and why we believe it, there arise forces independent of everything like mathematical demonstration. The truth is there is just this difference between facts and ideas. There are not the same kind of rules relating to ideas and abstract things which there are pertaining to facts. The consciousness of the Supreme Being, which is sometimes called a belief, sometimes a realisation, is believed or realised according to the mental attitude. It may be a matter which appears to have been demonstrated by the testimony of others, or it may be one of personal experience. A person who knows himself to have passed through, we will say, the experience of prayer, that is, to have felt that he was once in communion with the Deity, may reasonably regard the evidence of a Divine Presence as a matter of experience, and therefore independent of the testimony of others. The Psalmist who wrote, "When I cried unto Thee, Thou answeredst me, and strengthenedst me with strength in my soul," was clearly recording what, to his mind, appeared as an experience. He was not supplying the logical inference of any proposition, nor the result of the testimony of another. He was just stating what he had seen, as it were, in the same way as a man might announce that he had witnessed a particular scene, or had felt a certain physical sensation. This was an experience. To the person who wrote those words the evidence of the Divine Being was essentially a matter within his own personal experience. He had felt the strength with which he had been strengthened in his soul. That person might have been quite indifferent to any argument, however sound, which could establish the proposition that there was a God. He knew there was a God of his own knowledge, because he had experienced something which he had received by reason of a communion with that Being.

The dangers of this argument of experiences will be manifest to any critical mind. For different people testify that they have had opposite experiences on the same subject, and one person has experienced a different kind of Deity from another. A Christian will declare that he has experienced the in-dwelling of Christ, and a Mohammedan would not have had such an experience. Yet in face of this obvious danger we are not at liberty to deny that religious impressions are matters of experience. On the contrary, so certain is it that the strongest convictions are matters of experience and not merely of ordinary evidence, that we must accept the fact with all its risks and with all its dangers.

For purposes of argument there is certainly a distinction between true or imaginary experience, but for the purpose of human feeling and conduct the result is much the same. Moreover these two experiences—the Psalmist speaking of God and the Christian of Christ—may after all be but a difference of language rather than a difference of sense. The doctrines of different religions beyond the one touching the existence of God are such that the various people who believe them do so by reason of other influences than the one great force of experience. For example, particular dogmas respecting the authority of the Scriptures are certainly questions not of experience but of argument. And again, a belief in the immortality of the soul, from the nature of the case, is a subject about which there cannot be any human experience. The Jewish doctrine of the election of Israel, or the Christian doctrine of the Atonement, are of necessity matters which cannot come within the compass of individual experiences. They are essentially ideas which may be believed or not in consequence of other forces than that of experience—historical evidence in the one case, or metaphysical reasoning in the other; but nobody ever believed in either of them because he had experienced them. Perhaps there are very few points in religious thought which do come within that area of personal experience. In ethics there are several matters which may be experienced. Such, for instance, as remorse for sin, a tranquil conscience following worthy acts. And again, the emotions of love and hate, passion and calm, anger and reconciliation—these are distinctly facts within the horizon of personal experience.

Experience changes conviction. We do not reason upon subjects in which experience can play any part without reference to the part which it plays. Ill-cultivated minds form opinions without adequate regard to human experience either personal or historical. The average fireside politician, or church and chapel goer, regard their opinions very much in the way that they regard their style of dress. Habit formed them, habit retains them. New facts which come to light in the world of thought do not amend or modify the habitual believer in regard to politics or religion. They are not cognisant of these new facts.

Experience, regarded as a powerful element in the formation of opinions and beliefs, is the clue to the changes which take place in the views of thoughtful persons. It is an error to regard change of opinions as indications either of a weak intellect or of a wavering judgment. People of that kind either have no convictions, or if they possess them, they never change them. All people are not affected by experience in a like degree. Persons are often ill-prepared to take up into their lives the philosophical results of a new experience.

In practical affairs, experience is so conspicuously ignored as a teacher, that it is not surprising it should have so little effect in the abstract views of ordinary persons. It is amazing to observe how little impression is made upon the average man and woman by the ordinary experiences even in physical matters. The causes of a cold or a headache are known from personal experience to be generally preventible, yet colds and headaches recur again and again when they might be avoided, often from the selfsame cause. In the very elementary matter of the preparation of food, a cook without any scientific training in that department must by experience acquire the knowledge of such facts as the time needed to roast a joint of a certain weight, or to boil a potato. No doubt thousands of cooks, unmindful of this experience, repeatedly exceed or diminish the time which they might have observed to be indispensable.

The loss of knowledge to be obtained from experiences may be accounted for by the want of cultivating the powers of observation. People allow themselves to go through life mentally blindfold. Facts pass before them unseen, unperceived, just like the succession of wonderful scenes in the firmament pass day by day and year by year unappreciated, because unnoticed by the optical vision of the Goth. Many persons are indifferent to the changes of the weather, and have never made a mental note of the experience that a south-westerly wind brings rain, and that a northerly one carries cold. If due note had been made of these experiences one might have learnt from them something of weather changes.

"The burnt child dreads the fire," is a very

simple illustration of experience working upon the mind. The property of heat has in that case been ascertained entirely by personal experience. There are large fields of knowledge attainable by experience, if only one were to employ the faculty of observation. Absent-mindedness, or not noticing facts which surround us, is probably the reason why so much knowledge is missed and experience lost. Observation may be quickened by practice. The current events of ordinary lives can be interpreted through the light which experience will shed upon them. Some most difficult cases of what are called exceptional circumstances are rendered intensely confusing for want of the knowledge of some similiar case. One man of experience will come to the solution of a highly controverted and complex problem by reason of having watched in a past experience the working of a like issue. All known theories may fail to account for these strange incidents, and unless some one in the crowd of onlookers has once witnessed such a scene before, and tested the effects of particular action, hopeless chaos is likely to prevail.

It is highly probable that experience is the principal factor in the efficiency of medical practice. The same truth applies to other professions. The homely saying that "practice makes perfect" is a way of expressing the power of experience. Practice means repeated experiences. Some of the best organists are persons with eyesight so defective that they cannot read the names of the stops, which are generally inscribed in dazzling old English. Experience enables them to know which stops to use and which to avoid.

Experience is closely connected with the faculty of memory. Persons of weak memory naturally forget what they have seen and known. There are certain experiences, however, which impress themselves in a physical way, leaving their influence apart from the recollected or forgotten incidents which gave rise to them. Such for example are the experiences of heat and cold, hunger and sleep, pleasure and pain, sickness and health. Knowledge of those sensations is stamped upon every individual by the sheer force of experience. The experience of them is so vivid, and the knowledge of them so complete, that the events with which they were connected may fade from the memory and yet the experience remains. In such cases the fact of frequent recurrence in some instances, like the sensations of hunger and sleep, regularly and systematically, is enough to render effects impressionable apart from their causes. The effects remain while the cause is lost. Yet all this belongs to the subject of experience. What is known or ascertainable even by men of science with regard to the sensations mentioned is quite insignificant in comparison with the knowledge of them derived from experience.

When we say that some things are so obvious that they do not need reasoning about, we are describing the all-powerful attribute of experience. What are called platitudes and truisms are things which lie positively within the experience of everyone, unless they be fallacies. Oft repeated utterances which are not true do bear the semblance of reality until they are discovered to be false. A great deal of experience is lost for practical purposes in consequence of false reasoning about facts Wrongheadedness and perverted judgment obscure the lesson which experience would teach in regard to a given group of facts. John Stuart Mill has plainly shown that plurality of causes may bewilder the human mind in searching for the particular cause in a given case. Theory and fact appear often to be in opposition to one another. But it is only an appearance if the theory be true. For in that case the fact would be misapprehended. Far more likely, however, that a theory has been set up against a fact with which it is irreconcileable. Here people would be arguing on a false premise. They may have had an experience out of which the theory was conceived, but it happened not to be the experience exactly similar to the case in dispute. If life were long enough to admit the possibility of reading the details of every law suit that has taken place within a generation, and it were possible to retain a recollection of them, the average man would discover a mine of experience that could not otherwise have come within the range of his personal career. Many theories would fly to the winds, theories that had hitherto been regarded as unquestionably true. This is why the services of experts and specialists are valuable for the elucidation of various difficulties. When we speak of some one having a special knowledge of a particular matter, what we mean is, that in reference to the subject he has had opportunities of experience which have not fallen to others. The reason why it is more difficult to treat internal diseases is just the want of experience owing to the hidden source of complaint and consequent difficulty of observation.

Experience cannot be dissociated from observation. It would be like fishing without bait or tackle. The reason, therefore, why experience has a greater effect upon one person than upon another is that he possesses a stronger power of observation. Everybody has experience, but all are not equally equipped with the faculty to observe. It may safely be contended that observation is the most considerable factor in the acquisition of knowledge and of proficiency in science, in painting, in music, and in almost every department of study. For what is study of any given subject if it be not a placing of the student in such relations with his subject that he has the fullest opportunity of accumulating experiences in regard to it? Every candidate for the Oxford

EXPERIENCE.

School of Literæ Humaniores and for the Cambridge Mathematical tripos has the same material before him in each case. That is to say whether it be in mathematics or in classics and philosophy, there are certain books which must be read. In other words, certain specific experiences are by the reading of these books placed before the mental vision like so many lenses of a magic lantern. The man who comes out at the head of the list and the man who comes out last have each passed through the same experiences, or rather the same experiences have passed before them. The difference in the result is due, therefore, not to varied experiences but to unequal observation. All has been observed in the one case, only a part has been observed in the other. It may be urged here that some other quality besides observation plays a part in the acquisition of knowledge, namely a retentive memory. But a retentive memory without observation would be unavailable. One might almost define the essence of genius to be an extraordinary endowment of the power of observation. In other words, what is done by observation precedes and underlies what is accomplished by the memory. And both these mental processes operate upon the field of experience.

And, coming to memory, what is known as learning by heart is surely an achievement effected by an intellectual contract between the two attributes of experience and observation. Memory, indeed, is that attribute of the human mind which is the storehouse of a manufacture woven together by the two previous intellectual looms. There would be nothing to remember, however great was the gift of memory, except for what had taken place between experience and observation.

TACT.

THE definition of extremes is simpler than the definition of qualities which are more or less co-relative. Everybody comprehends in a moment what is meant by the North and South Pole as a figure of speech. The truth is that throughout the domain of human character there are very few, if any, sharp lines of cleavage between one set of attributes and another. There is, however, the most marked and striking contrast between those qualities which lie at the extreme points. Thus it is easier to describe a genius and a fool, than it is to delineate two persons of moderate but varied intelligence. It may also be found that there is no line drawn in nature which divides good from evil, strong from weak, sane from insane, &c. There is no doubt as to the extreme cases at either end of the column. There are, then, a large number scattered at various points between the two ends.

So in the consideration of any matter touching character, it is best to form a clear conception of the opposite extremes. This question of tact is a far weightier and more subtle element in social relations than may be supposed. Tact, in its highest form, can only be exhibited by a person of the highest intelligence, while the total absence of the quality is to be experienced in intercourse with people of very meagre understanding. Tact is dependent upon a high development of the powers of imagination, and these powers vary in the same proportion as the general mental capacity of mankind.

Tact, in its lower forms, is sometimes nothing above the art of deception springing from mean and selfish devices. On the other hand, in its higher manifestations, it is one of the noblest virtues. Tact can represent selfishness and unselfishness, sympathy and antipathy, love and hatred. But for no purpose and in no case can it be exercised without some degree of mental ability. Tact is primarily an intellectual quality, though its exercise is dependent upon the moral attributes. No element, perhaps, in human character, presents a more interesting proof of the close connection between the moral and the intellectual qualities, and also their distinct separateness, than tact.

Yes, it is a great subject which lies behind that little word of four letters. There opens up to us the whole avenue through which we might stroll if we attempt to enter the fields of mental and moral philosophy.

The majority of persons are superficial. They are superficial in education and in thought. This accounts for the vague and loose notions to be met with in human intercourse. Ordinary people, who compose the bulk of every population, might regard tact, like manners, as something of very little significance, and altogether external, having no connection with the real springs of human character. It is doubtful whether there is one trainer of young persons in a thousand to whom it would appear essential to give instructions about tact or about manners.

Tact is essentially a subordination of self in an unselfish consideration of others. No rules could be laid down to teach a person how to exercise it. Like many of the most precious graces and talents, it is mainly an attribute of the temperament, and is exercised unconsciously; still it may, in a useful measure, be acquired and cultivated by people of moderate intelligence. Imagination, quick and subtle, is the strong power which is found to underlie every character that has any charm about it. A person not gifted with imagination, or endowed only in a very sparing degree, cannot wield tact. It is no fault of his. The best he can do is to hold his tongue when he would propose to advise or to console his neighbours. Say nothing, unless you are perfectly sure that you can say the right thing. In no way is tact more strongly demanded than in forming a correct judgment at a moment's notice on the question of your competence, then and there, to advise or to console. Flow of words, either in connection with consolation or advice, is generally a dangerous exploit. Yet there are cases in which it is a success; and there are many instances in which a prolonged silence indicates the want of tact. Silence, though not always silvern, is not always golden. It is very often no better than leaden. Persons who flatter themselves on their power of keeping silent, are of very mixed multitude. Silence is a way of escaping a great many things, both good as well as evil. Timely speech, accurate speech, tender speech, are, on the other hand, useful, generous, and human. The first shock of pain which we experience in the presence of our beloved dead is their speechlessness. Speech is in reality the only vital medium of sympathy and happiness. And that kind of silence, which is sometimes a comfort, is only the silence of a sort which partakes of messages understood as though they were expressed. A bright smile, a certain look from one to another, which is of any use, is the smile and the look which actually represents ideas, or emotions that are capable of being uttered. The abstinence from utterance in such a case is due, probably, not to the want of speech, but to the desire to impart the idea in some less usual way. There is a difference between what is commonly known as "talking" and speech.

A silent companion is to most properly constituted people an insufferable bore after the first day. Even that day was a long one when I took a journey with X., who never said anything from

Calais to Geneva, except "All right," and to tell me the time. The whole value of silence, that exaggerated commodity of such doubtful value, is that it should be available only when required. But silence, at times when it is not needed, is more tiresome than speech, because you cannot say to the silent man "Leave off." He never leaves off. And there can be no variety in his entertainment. Oh, that silent man! He is one of three things: a cynic, a villain, or an imbecile. And what difference can there be to his companion which of those three things he happens to be? In outward aspect they are the same. Silence means something more besides abstaining from speech. It means an awkward occasional "No."

So much for silence. Tactlessness in speech is more frequent. And perhaps there is more often a conscious difficulty in saying the right thing at the proper time than in maintaining a silence. Many persons foolishly imagine that it is necessary to say something—no matter what. It is a good plan to take breathing time, and consider duly what should be said. This seems a mere commonplace, yet how few there are who think of pausing for such a purpose. Clumsy speech, silly remarks, unasked advice, are often manifestations of want of tact. A particular observation which is perfectly innocent from the point of view of the speaker—perhaps only a vague proposition applicable to many cases—ought to be considered, before it is uttered, in reference to its probable effect upon the person addressed. Here much thought is required for the exercise of tact. Then again there are methods of conveying ideas less objectionable than others. Speaking in an abstract sense may be sometimes found a valuable way of imparting an opinion; on the other hand, speaking *at* a person is to be avoided. That is invariably irritating. Some persons prefer direct personal appeals to innuendoes.

In the matter of making jokes, great tact may be exercised, or tact may be conspicuous by its absence. It is not because a joke is a good one *per se*, that it is a desirable joke on a given occasion, or that it is suitable for the hearing of certain individuals. A man of tact who is given to making jokes is a very different person from a tactless individual who is also given to joking. A true insight into character is necessary before the man of humour can exercise his wit with advantage. Such a person can see in a moment whether his favourite joke is likely to fall flat, or to have an enlivening effect. As the effect of a joke—indeed, the very apprehension of a joke—depends entirely upon the character of the audience and of their present mood, it requires quick intelligence and perception to find what those moods are. It may often be observed that the same joke produces opposite impressions upon different people. One will enjoy a hearty laugh over it, another will gape, and a third will scowl, or they will laugh, gape, or scowl on different occasions.

It is an error on the part of a witty man to suppose that because a joke is excellent, or a story is worth telling, it is excellent for all people, and worth telling on all occasions.

In no circumstance is tact more difficult than in visiting the sick or bereaved. Careful avoidance of the cause of pain or sorrow is in some cases an exercise of tact; in others it is quite tactless. Here again the character, and the mood of the person visited, have to be considered. Hence to make a rule for all cases implies a want of wisdom and an absence of tact. Some people are comforted by allusions to their trouble or even conversation about it; others prefer that the matter should not be broached. The practice of conducting one's conversation by means of asking questions is a singularly untactful one. It does not always imply what it professes, that the questioner feels a true interest in the affairs of the questioned victim. Quite the reverse; idle curiosity is often at the bottom of these interrogatory conversations. On occasions of sickness or sorrow questions are more than usually trying and unpleasant. The invalid or bereaved may not have the bodily strength or the mental vigour to evade the questions as he could do at ordinary times. Some of these questions may have the effect of extracting from him something which ought not to be imparted to another. Even the compulsion of uttering a simple yes or no may give the clue to a matter which ought to have been kept secret. The conventional query,

"Do you feel better to-day?" is harmless enough and perfectly natural, but when it is followed with minute inquiries, it is sometimes injurious for the very person whom it is sought to console. It is usually a mistake to ask an invalid what kind of nourishment he is taking, except by the medical attendant, and then it is best to put the question to some one else. "How did you sleep last night?" or "have you had a good night?" is a very common way of beginning a conversation with elderly people, but an indiscreet one. It is equally foolish in the case of invalids. Sleeplessness is increased by contemplating it. Most of us have experienced at some time the horror of insufficient sleep, and we know therefore that the more we think of it the worse it generally becomes. A curious story is told of a distinguished physician who has passed away. He was singularly gifted with tact. His practice was one of the largest of his time. He possessed the faculty of making a patient feel that he was never in a hurry, and that the particular case before him was all in all for the time being. He was called in consultation to an hysterical lady who had no specific complaint, The family doctor informed him that she had some sixteen questions to ask about her condition, that she had written them down in order. Whilst the lady was going through the questions the physician was quietly taking her temperature and pulse, and by the time she arrived at No. 3, the visit ended without the lady having the slightest notion that the physician had not listened to the entire sixteen. She was, moreover, charmed by the physician's courteous bearing and general attention to her case.

Visits to people who are labouring under the stress of exceptional events such as those already indicated, and many others, may elicit a degree of tact carefully prepared for the special occasion, which are not at all times available. Hence it is desirable to consider the exercise of tact in ordinary circumstances. George Eliot has pointed out in another connection that some people are particularly kind when you break your leg, but then you do not break your leg every day, and at ordinary times these persons are rather unpleasant.

Now there are what may be termed eccentricities in human intercourse in which tact is quite out of sight. We have all met with individuals who pride themselves on being what they term "very outspoken," and who flatter themselves that they are exceptionally honest and straightforward, because they always say what they think. To be outspoken and to say always what one thinks is a proceeding which entails a great deal that renders the society of these honest folk truly obnoxious. There is a fallacy in the reasoning of such persons with regard to the claims of truth. As a matter of fact most of the things which they say of the "outspoken" category are invariably such things as have no relation whatever to abstract truth, but merely to their own personal idiosyncrasies. Egotism and conceit are more frequently the cause of this outspokenness than any genuine love of truth. People have an undoubted right to think what they like about others, but there is no inherent right in human nature to communicate those thoughts. A and B meet one another. B is outspoken. A is reticent. B informs A that someone else whom B does not personally know, but who is an intimate friend of A, is a villain or a fool. That is outspoken, but not necessarily true. It is after all only the impression of B formed on probably insufficient evidence. Perhaps A will vindicate his friend, and tell B he thinks So-and-so is bad because he does not know him, and assure B that the individual is anything but a fool or a villain. Then B replies that A is only speaking from the prejudices of a friend, and cannot form a judgment. Some outspoken people can become positively insulting in the mere exercise of ordinary conversation. And not only in speaking of persons can the outspoken individual be objectionable. Whether conversation turns on books, on politics, on art, or any imaginable topic, if he insists upon saying always what he thinks without reference to the thoughts of others, he is bound to display the characteristics of an insufferable bore. The supposed merit of that outspokenness is a popular fallacy. The charm of human intercourse cannot exist where people give annoyance to one another. Of course there is the widest possible difference between saying what you think and saying what you do not think. The one is obviously not the only alternative of the other. It is a good rule not to vouchsafe what you think on ordinary topics unless your thoughts are solicited, and then they can be conveyed in a manner that is not at all unpleasant. The outspoken creature is invariably unpleasant. Another excellent principle of social intercourse is to minimise differences of opinion as far as possible, and in no case to exaggerate them.

True tact, far from being a mere outward mannerism, proceeds from a genuine love of our species. It is connected with the finest feelings, and is the outcome of unselfishness. To save people from embarrassment of all kinds, to relieve them from anything like pressure in their communications, and to render them quite at their ease, are indications of a high cultivation of this quality. The private circumstances of intimate friends vary enormously, and it is between persons who associate on a footing of sincere friendship, in which tact is most urgently required, and sometimes difficult to attain. The popular idea that you can say anything to a person with whom you are on intimate terms is an error of judgment. However intimate you may be, a certain reserve is desirable, at least in relation to matters which concern himself and not yourself. With regard to your own concerns, you are at liberty to seek his confidence, and to tell him what you please about yourself, but not about his affairs. It is a great mistake to suppose that tact can be dispensed with in the intercourse between intimate friends and near relatives. This supposition is the cause of many a breach and of much domestic unhappiness. Neither the closest ties of friendship or of blood should properly absolve people from a thorough and careful regard to the natural independence of each human being. Some persons are by nature more communicative than others, and some families live on terms of greater confidence than others. We occasionally hear of people living together who have no secrets from one another. This is somewhat rare, if we come to think about it. And even where such relations exist, tact should still remain a vital element in their intercourse.

There is much difference of opinion with regard to what are termed confidences. Yet it is apparent that the confidence which one individual reposes in another carries with it high obligations. The knowledge thus acquired must be put away in the confided heart as though it were not there. The notion that husbands and wives may convey to one another what they have learnt in that manner is utterly unsound and unwarranted. Marriage is a condition in which the exercise of tact is of paramount consequence. If it were possible to investigate the causes of marriage failures, it might be discovered that tactlessness plays a conspicuous part. The tie of marriage carries with it not only no absolution from the necessity for tact, but makes very special claims upon it. Those couples who are most devoted to each other, yet need the habitual display of tact, if they mean to preserve a continuous state of happiness. Many pairs who are said to be happily married, and who, on the whole, live peacefully together, are at times subject to a certain tension. And those times are by no means infrequent. Probably they occur several times in one week. A great many men and women are really unfit for married life just because they have no tact. Marriage being the condition which places two persons on terms of greatest confidence is probably the one that calls for the greatest exercise of tact. In other words, this quality is of so much significance in its effect upon human intercourse, that the urgency of its claim increases rather than diminishes according to the degrees of intimacy between one human soul and another. People are likely to imagine that tact is chiefly required in the intercourse between persons of slight acquaintance. That is a shallow view of the matter. Self-interest in the worldly affairs will be some inducement to be tactful in business intercourse among men and women of the world. To get on in life, tact is indispensable; but to insure perfect happiness in the domestic circle and in private friendship, this quality becomes elevated to the level of an endearing virtue. There is generally one member of the family who is more endowed with tact than the rest of them. He or she will, therefore, be the peacemaker and the wise counsellor. In conclusion, it will be found that those persons who are most lovable and most gifted in their personal qualities, possess, in a high degree, the virtue of tact.

THE PULPIT, ITS DEFECTS, ITS POSSIBILITIES.

THE failure of preachers to produce the effect upon society which their exceptional opportunities might enable them to do, is a problem worthy of consideration. This failure might be attributed to many causes, but it is proposed here to consider only two. It will be seen that these two are dependent one on the other. It may be well to lay some claim to a proof of the proposition that on the whole there is that failure.

In the first place, it will be admitted that throughout Great Britain the clergy in all denominations are a body of speakers and writers, who have a more regular and larger public to address than any other class of spokesmen or authors. With the single exception of members of Parliament of Cabinet rank, no public man, and certainly very few men of letters, can at all times command the large sympathetic audiences, and the frequent opportunities of public utterance which are at the disposal of preachers. It could not be contended that the opportunities even of statesmen for instructing and edifying their fellow-countrymen are so numerous and diverse as those of the clergymen. For the politician is confined to one range of topic, and he is not at liberty to travel out of the sphere of practical politics. He is expected to speak on some specific question which at the time is interesting, if not agitating, the public mind. Selection of a subject is hardly given to him, because it is determined by the exigencies of the political situation. His audiences do not include in any large proportion either women or children; moreover, the men who compose the bulk of his audiences already share his convictions, or are present to oppose them. However able the addresses of a statesman may be, they are immediately subject to the negative influences of party debate and journalistic criticism. It rarely happens that either the Prime Minister or the leader of the Opposition has anything to say which is not at once contradicted and undermined by another speaker of equal prominence. Not so with a minister of religion; he is seldom contradicted or criticised; his audiences are generally friendly and include people of both sexes, all ages, and varied capacity, ever ready to believe what he says, and to appreciate the smallest display of talent. Leaders of men, both statesmen and men of letters, go to hear him if he is at all above the average. It must therefore be admitted that his opportunities are very remarkable. In face of these opportunities nobody can deny that the general result is insignificantly disproportionate.

The two reasons referred to are difficult to place in their correct order; one is that the average preacher is intellectually below the average literary man or statesman; the other that he invariably addresses himself to subjects which do not palpably concern the interests of society. In other words, he wastes his opportunities. He discourses upon topics of which it may be said that they have more interest for another world than for this one. Here it is necessary to meet a logical difficulty which will at once be raised by any number of divines who might read these words. They would say in a loud chorus that it is just those matters which relate to another sphere that have the most direct concern for people in this one. That is of course an hypothesis which, if true, would dispose of the proposition that preaching does not accomplish the most that might fairly be expected of it.

Human nature, however, whether the preachers see it or not, is actually more concerned with the affairs of its transitory life than it is with those of the future state.

Any one who has heard a great many sermons must have experienced that very few of them attempt to deal with the problems which affect the ordinary human relations of every-day life.

It would be unfair to put out of sight what may be called the trammels of the preacher, or to deny the causes which put a limit on the range of subjects with which it is customary for him to deal. Still it is just such fetters which it is well to criticise, not by any means holding the preachers as a class entirely responsible for the drawbacks of their office. Conventionality is perhaps more answerable for those restrictions than anything else, and it is this conventionality which has to be resisted. People go to church to hear a sermon about a text or in justification of a doctrine; they are amazed and open-mouthed when by chance they hear anything else. The preacher and his congregation seem to co-operate in maintaining the hindrances of the pulpit to the detriment of both.

The occasion of a sermon or an address in a place of worship, attended as it is by every circumstance of seriousness and reflection, affords a most fitting opportunity to say to the people that which cannot well be conveyed on any other occasion, yet how much there is which is never said at all. Hundreds and thousands of sermons are wasted upon the consideration of matters which do not touch the improvement of society, the spread of culture, or the cultivation of better human relations. Take, for example, what is known as a fashionable congregation in the West of London at the height of the season. Here is a concourse of prosperous persons, assembled to do what? First, of course, to worship God, then to listen and to be morally improved—the utmost that they are likely to receive in the way of elevation, will be in connection with an occasional appeal from the pulpit on behalf of a charity. Then, at least, they are called upon to exercise in some degree that "very bond of peace and of all virtues." The preacher, if he be a man of the world, possessing any knowledge of the ways of society, must be aware that his audience is composed, to a large extent, of men and women whose habits of life include much of the sham, the insincerities and the grotesque vanities which pervade the world of fashion.

There is not one sermon in a hundred which alludes to such subjects. They are all on passages in the Epistles or about the central doctrines of the popular creed, which is supposed to be compatible with the existing order of social life. It is rarely that we hear sermons on genuineness or friendship. The divorce of politics from religion is not often deplored in the pulpit. The development of the intellect, and the value of art, are seldom extolled from that edifice. The absorbing questions of social reform, the equalisation of human opportunities, and the removal of artificial inequalities—questions deeply touching the very springs of moral action and the well-being of our species—where is the preacher who would venture to touch upon them? "The pulpit is not the place to discuss politics," is a conventional remark which these observations might elicit. This is one of the fundamental popular errors in respect to sermons and the ends they ought to have in view. If, as is admitted, the object of preaching is the improvement of society, it is difficult to understand why so many limitations should be placed around the pulpit. If, on the other hand, the purpose was nothing but to set forth certain ecclesiastical dogmas, the present system is at least intelligible. So also are its results. But it seems worth while to refute this conception of the office of the pulpit. Teach what you like in your catechism, but do not waste the golden opportunity of the preacher.

Whilst it must be admitted that the average talent, both literary and rhetorical, of preachers in general is of moderate degree, the exceptions are more numerous than are commonly supposed. The majority of candidates for the House of Commons and of those who go there, are decidedly worse speakers than the majority of clergymen. Their total culture is considerably less. Public men who are really good speakers both in and out of Parliament do not muster a heavy roll. And those who excel above that standard, and might be described as orators, are so few that they may be counted on the fingers. In point of composition, the average clergyman of the Church of England is by no means inferior.

Among the various Nonconformist bodies, the minister of the Gospel has attained a degree of excellence in extempore speaking, which will compare favourably with the rhetorical accomplishments of Members of Parliament. In the House of Lords fewer members take part in the debate than in the House of Commons, and a higher degree of merit is attained in the Upper

Chamber. This is easy to account for. Few people feel under any compulsion to make a speech in the House of Peers. Those who do so honestly believe that they have something to say, and they are obviously less under the demoralising influence of popular judgment.

Among the clergy of all denominations there are a considerable number of men who speak particularly well; there are not a few who display rare gifts of eloquence and occasional flights of oratory. Nonconformist ministers, even of the rugged and itinerant type, sometimes exhibit striking powers of speech. It might be observed not infrequently that the most effective speaker at a Parliamentary election meeting was the man who had been an habitual preacher of the Gospel. Since the removal of University tests, and the general progress of national education, Dissenting ministers have made a more marked stride in the art of public speaking than is noticeable among the clergy of the Established Church, or the Roman Catholic Church, within the same period. This superiority is largely due to the fact that conventionality in the structural form of a sermon is much less observed among Dissenting bodies than in the two older Churches. The reason for this difference as to method and treatment is in a measure owing to the freedom of Dissenters from ecclesiastical supervision. It is probable that the triumph of Puritanism during the Commonwealth and the progress of Dissenting sects in our own time, have been considerably aided by the greater freedom of speech which has obtained in the chapel. Few people can deny, if they have considered the subject, that the average sermon in the Church of England, in spite of the correctness of composition, is a thoroughly stereotyped production. Neither in its subject nor in its arrangement is there any play of the imagination; moreover, the dulness of bad delivery, answering to prescribed ritual regulation, varying between a monotone and a drawl, is calculated to mar even the reading of a well-written essay.

Here are some of the types of ordinary sermons. There is the elucidation of a particular text delivered by a man who has persistently abstained throughout his career from making himself acquainted with the work and the results of historical criticism. He is quite uninformed as to anything of consequence which scholars may have had to say upon the text itself or upon the book or chapter from which it is probably but a disjointed phrase. The first thing this clergyman sets about, after repeating the quotation two or three times to enable him to accent different words, is to refer to some other passages in different parts of the Scriptures which present to his uncritical mind points of similarity. If he is a very high churchman he will next proceed to tell the congregation what St. Augustine and Thomas Aquinas thought about the passage.

He may mention some other commentators, but they are sure to be those only who lived and thought in an age when scientific criticism was unknown. His third process is to read into the words some meaning, which from the nature of the case was never in the mind of the original author, insisting of course on the peculiar subtlety of the sacred writings, by which it is to be understood that you can make a sentence mean anything you please. His particular meaning will depend upon the exact order of his churchmanship, whether high, low, or broad, in their different degrees. The words "Verily, verily" have been discussed in this fashion. So also "Render unto Cæsar that which is Cæsar's," and a vast number of others.

In the Roman Catholic Church, a part of a sentence from the Psalms, such as, "Thou art the queen" ("of Ophir," being carefully omitted) has formed the basis of a discourse upon the feast of the Assumption. "And Jesus said unto His disciples" is a favourite groundwork of a sermon in churches of various denominations. Then there is the Evangelical sermon quite different from any other except in its tendency to play upon words and to fix the attention upon matters distinctly removed from the ordinary affairs of life.

There is the sermon about a Biblical personage of whom nothing is known except a fragmentary description in the sacred text. Of course there are countless sermons upon themes suggested by the great celebrations of the Church, such as Christmas, Easter, and Whitsuntide. The dogmas which these commemorations emphasise are separately treated on most of the Sundays in the year. In Evangelical churches the Atonement, the Resurrection and the Ascension, and the doctrine of hell, as well as the verbal inspiration in the entire body of Scriptures, form the main topics for sermons. In High churches, the subjects are varied by such points as the Eucharist, the Real Presence, and the rest of the Church ordinances. In Broad churches these matters are but lightly touched upon, and of course, quite differently.

There are sermons without number which treat of various incidents mentioned in the Books of the Old and New Testaments, having little or no connection whatever with the problems of our own times. The attempt to whitewash the conduct of Jacob in that revolting act of deception practised upon his aged father has been heard often enough in every place of worship. The early chapters of Genesis abound in favourite topics for all kinds of preachers. The Books of Psalms and Proverbs, perhaps the most suggestive for spiritual and ethical treatment, are much less frequently used. The Epistles of Paul are more commonly taken for texts than any passage in the Sermon on the Mount.

There are, undoubtedly, in this body of writings, very precious materials for homily. But it is curious to note there are fewer sermons preached

THE PULPIT, ITS DEFECTS, ITS POSSIBILITIES. 63

from such a text as "Husbands love your wives, and be not bitter against them," than others like the famous passage in the Epistle to the Romans: "Know ye not that so many of us as were baptised into Jesus Christ were baptised into His death." The disposition to select mystical passages rather than those which are palpably intelligible is very remarkable indeed. The Books of Daniel and Ezekiel, and the Acts of the Apostles and Revelations are more often chosen to discourse upon than any of the simpler utterances of the Hebrew Prophets or of the Apostles.

The extraordinary wealth of language and of ideas belonging to the Bible certainly renders that vast collection a sufficient storehouse from which to gather priceless teaching, but the best of them are seldom used. There are never sermons delivered without a text, and yet how rarely is it well chosen. Some of the better class of preachers employ a quotation merely as a peg on which to hang the discourse; it serves the twofold purpose of paying homage to the authority of Scripture and of diffusing ideas upon all questions touching the deeper truths of ethics and religion.

Most of that which is spoken from the pulpit falls immeasurably short of what might be said. No one is at liberty, like the preacher, to be so outspoken in public. He is privileged to address his fellow-countrymen upon the most sacred questions about which he can think. He may tell multitudes the secret ways of spiritual happiness. He may speak also of the hindrances to those ways, of the moral blemishes in common life; and he can tell about the means by which better paths may be trodden, and a nobler career secured. He may advise, too, on some of those subtle relations in human affairs which touch deeply the domestic happiness of men and women. If the preacher be a man of originality, and is capable of true discernment, he would see at a glance how closely the intellectual and the spiritual life are interwoven, and how the two react upon one another.

The sacred right to education, and the value of general culture, are questions which did not find their way into the pulpit in a previous generation. It cannot be said that the pulpit lent its powerful aid to the awakening of public opinion about the cause of national elementary education, nor, indeed in any of those great measures enacted within the present century for the amelioration of unjust suffering and for the redress of undeserved grievances. Was William Wilberforce largely supported by the Anglican pulpit in his crusade against slavery? The pulpit was not at the service of those who, within the last twenty-five years, have obtained from Parliament legislative amendment in the conditions of the factory and the work-shop. Much loss of power on the part of the pulpit is due, no doubt, to the lack of concerted effort.

In the several struggles for the improvement of the condition of the working classes, by no means

THE PULPIT, ITS DEFECTS, ITS POSSIBILITIES. 65

ended yet, it is obvious that, were anything like united effort on the part of preachers of all denominations seriously undertaken, they could muster a far stronger agency for directing aright the action of the modern democracy than anything that can be expected from the efforts of mere party agitators.

But no! there is the preposterous conventional dogma that the preacher must only talk about a text and theology, and never about politics or social problems. Unhappily, the clergy are too much of a profession, and, therefore, not sufficiently an independent moral force. This, again, is owing to a mistaken popular view in regard to them.

The first sign of an improved state of things, showing what the pulpit is capable of effecting, may be seen by the results of the recent institution of "Hospital Sunday." This, no doubt, is the single example of it, and that it works admirably, no one would deny. If public meetings were called on behalf of the hospitals it is doubtful whether they would produce such satisfactory results as the pulpit movement. Those effects are not only excellent from the point of view of the hospital treasurer, but they contribute in a high degree to the moral culture of the public. If this system were extended to other questions of public utility a large amount of good would accrue both socially and morally. Some of the Dissenting bodies have already given conspicuous proof of the power which the pulpit can wield in that vital working-man's question of temperance.

There are many crises in the affairs of a nation when alternative policies are submitted by politicians, but never by the clergy. The suggestion that they should participate in party strife is far from the intention of this article. Rather should their position be above and beyond the influences of party organisation, for the very reason that they should be in a position to declare, as from a height, the true moral significance attaching to the support of one political programme or another. When questions of peace or war arise out of the errors sometimes incidental to diplomatic transactions, or in consequence of wild journalistic venture, then it is that the pulpit could raise its voice to stay popular clamour, to allay public anxiety, and even to claim a fair hearing for the rights of the case. Likewise, with serious fluctuations of commerce and the consequent disquiet in the labour markets, the pulpit might exercise a more direct influence because it is above parties and the personal interests immediately in strife. It might have been well to have heard what the pulpit had to say on many of the recent strikes, in which the abstract cause of right and wrong were directly involved. There is, moreover, the problem of the relation between the Christian Socialism of the Gospels, and some ill-considered theories of our own times, about which the pulpit is silent.

In short, if we could get rid of conventionalities

in respect to the office of the pulpit, and there were a wider interpretation of the object of sermons, the advantages of preaching might be immeasurably increased. With less sacerdotalism than is apparent in the present system, and freer exercise of the intellectual faculties, the public might derive much more good than they do now. It should be remembered that for large numbers of people, sermons are all that they hear in the way of public speaking. This is the case not only in country districts but among many sections of the population in London and other large cities.

The present method of church preaching is subject to certain defects that it is worth while to mention. First, the excessive frequency with which a clergyman is required to preach is detrimental to his own power of doing so. It dries up the resources of his intellect, which his other duties leave little time to replenish.

A man would be an intellectual Hercules indeed who could regularly compose a sermon even once a week worth hearing. And yet there are thousands of clergymen who actually produce two or three. It is worthy of note that the most eminent preachers of our time deliver comparatively few sermons. It is questionable whether so great a master of pulpit homily as the ever-lamented Dr. Liddon would have produced fifty-two sermons in the year equal in merit to the twelve which were the limit of his discourses in St. Paul's.

Secondly, it may be urged that joining together the two functions of a sermon and a long service is undesirable both for the preacher and for those who listen to him. The sermon might with advantage be detached from the public worship, or annexed only to those services which are very short. The University Sermons at Oxford and Cambridge gain by the fact that people go for the sole purpose of hearing them, and that there is little else to listen to. Although their duration is longer than an ordinary sermon they produce much less dreariness for that reason. Such alterations in the conditions of a sermon are small in themselves, and perhaps they are scarcely worth the experiment so long as the present method of preaching is maintained. If, however, a new era of preaching and a new standard of sermons should come to pass, these details of change will be important.

If preaching is to approach to anything like a resemblance of the orations of the Hebrew prophets, the example which they set of speaking on the question of the day, and upon the pressing social and moral problem, must be widely followed. The result would be that the highest spiritual aims will be no more obscured than they were by the prophets of old.

MISSIONARY JUDAISM.

[" *Jewish Quarterly Review*," July, 1893.]

Is Judaism a missionary religion? Has it a propaganda? Are there possibilities that, beyond the confines of the Hebrew race, Judaism is capable of making itself felt as a religious system worthy of attracting people who are not of the "seed of Abraham"? These are questions which have been put again and again by Jews and non-Jews alike. The answers to them vary according to the precise meaning attached to the questions. One obvious, but superficial reply, is to say that for centuries it was as much as their lives were worth for the Jews in any part of the world to attempt a propaganda of their faith. That answer, although still the inevitable one so far as the Jews of such countries as Russia and Roumania are concerned, does not seem adequately to meet the question in respect to the Jews of England and America. Nor does it relate to the inquiry as to the missionary nature of Judaism. And it therefore becomes us to consider the question apart from circumstances of restraint, and apart also from the idea that Judaism is the religion of a single race. Placing out of sight the restrictions of circumcision and family heritage, we want to know whether the religion of Israel is one which embodies spiritual truths and ethical conceptions of a kind which are adaptable to the spiritual and ethical needs of men who are not of the race of Israel. In the following pages I desire to answer this question in the affirmative, and to endeavour to set forth grounds for the belief that there are aspects of the Jewish religion which may commend themselves to a vast number of Englishmen and Americans, and that it behoves English and American Jews who recognise these aspects to set them forth, and show them accordingly.

The present generation of English Christians (I use the word to signify non-Jews) has reached a stage of religious transition. There is distinct evidence of the fact that a large number of persons in this country, who have been christened in their infancy, do not hold fast to the doctrine of the Incarnation, or that of the Trinity. In other words, they do not any longer believe the fundamental dogmas of any of the organised forms of Christianity. Some of these people are Agnostics, many are Theists. It does not follow that dissent from orthodox Christianity is necessarily a separation from religion. The popular notion that there is no alternative between the religious beliefs of Christianity and no religion at all, is so palpably erroneous that it scarcely requires to be refuted. Judaism has undergone transitions too, in some respects similar to those through which Christianity is now passing. The difference, however, between the two cases of transition is of vital consequence, touching the subject upon which the change of view takes place. In Judaism, there is an undeniable modification of opinion in respect to matters of ritual, to rabbinical authority, and in reference to the restrictions required to maintain the identity of the Jewish people. But with regard to the nature of God, as to His oneness, His immutability, and incorporeality, there has been no change whatever. And as to the spiritual relations of the human and Divine, the religion of the Psalmists is still the religion of the modern Israelite, whether he be orthodox or reformer. In Christianity, on the other hand, the alteration of belief touches the nature of the Godhead and the theory of the relation between the Divine and the human. Fundamental dogma is here affected, whereas in Judaism the fundamental dogma remains undisturbed.

The Christian theory of atonement and "original sin" is the one which, probably, more than any other, differentiates Christianity from Judaism. It is necessary to notice this particular divergence between the two religions in order to consider whether Judaism presents a happier solution of the problem of sin than is offered by Apostolic teaching. The Christian dogmas on this subject postulate a kind of relationship between God and man which is not the same as that which is held in Judaism. The basis of any system of religion is undoubtedly something that belongs to the sphere of belief. And those persons who argue that Judaism is a system of observance only, and not of belief, are ignoring an elementary principle of human reason, namely, that practices must ultimately rest upon a belief. Now it is this fundamental belief, or basis, lying at the root of conduct and of faith, with regard to which Judaism and Christianity, in any of their respective forms, offer two distinct alternatives. Christianity is structurally built upon the hypothesis that, since the beginning of human history, mankind has been placed in a normal state of perdition. The event narrated in the legend of the Garden of Eden was that which brought sin and death into the world, and no human effort is capable of rescuing mankind, either individually or collectively, from the penalty of that great fall which is said to be historic. Then follows the superstructure in the vicarious atonement and the redeeming efficacy of blood by the sacrifice of "the Son of God." This, broadly speaking, is the essential dogma of every type of Christianity. There are, of course, the endless varieties, such as the different notions of the Greek and Latin Churches upon the subjects of the Trinity and the government of the Church; and then again the revolt of Protestantism against the Church of Rome upon the celebration of the great sacrifice, and the headship of the Church. But there is no body of Christians who are not parties to the teaching of the fall of man and salvation through Christ. To this teaching there has been no rival in any of the Christian communities of Europe and America upon any scale of numerical consequence. Christian Unitarianism is certainly a modification of the teaching, but it still adheres to the idea of a glorified Son of God in the person of Jesus. Within the present generation there has appeared a single clergyman, formerly of the Church of England, who has founded in London a Theistic Church, which definitely repudiates the theory of the Fall, and its consequent theory of redemption. Then there have appeared, from time to time, individuals, such as Bethune Inglish, and corporate bodies, who have repudiated Christianity and (some of them) Theism at once. And we have in London, Societies of Agnostics and the "Church of Humanity," founded on the principles of Auguste Comte, as well as a Society of Ethical Culture. But it cannot be said that there has been any missionary effort for teaching religion, that is, the worship of God and moral responsibility, upon the great historic foundation, such as that which Judaism embodies within her history and traditions.

The fact that there is among the educated classes of Englishmen and Americans, as well as among many who are not highly educated, a distinct and widespread repudiation of those fundamental Christian theories, suggests the question with which this article commenced: Is it possible that Judaism is capable of offering a solution to those who are not of the race of Israel? Such a question immediately suggests another: What aspect of

Judaism is it which is applicable to the religious needs of those who are not Jews? The difficulty at this point of the subject is, perhaps, less complicated than it appears to be. Judaism is a great historic testimony to the fact that men have worshipped God, have cherished faith, and acknowledged the claims of righteousness without believing in the Fall, and, therefore, without experiencing the necessity for miraculous redemption from that normal state of perdition. The testimony of this ancient and historic Theism has, without doubt, fallen to an hereditary group of people known as the People of Israel. The identity of this people has been preserved through thousands of years against incalculable difficulties. And the task of that preservation has imposed upon them obligations of a special and a peculiar kind. Special and peculiar, because their only purpose has been to preserve the group, and they lie quite apart from the great religious message which the Israelites have been treasuring. In proposing, therefore, that Israelites should teach what they know, it does not follow that they should teach those things which are only intended to preserve their communal identity. In such a propaganda of the Jewish faith we have only to consider those elements which are perfectly universalist in their character and their application. Distinctive rites, such as circumcision, eating of unleavened bread, dietary laws, and the particularity of the day for Sabbath observance are, from the nature of the case, institutions which do not possess any important significance for persons who are not hereditary members of the House of Israel. Sacred as many observances of this character appear to Jewish people, their sanctity is of a kind which owes its inspiration to the sense of family tradition rather than to any intrinsic solemnity, such as that which attaches to the practices of giving alms and of worshipping the Deity. The sanctity of such observances as those to which I refer are, of course, greatly enhanced in the minds of those members of the Jewish race who regard them as being not only family traditions, but also as the revealed will of God. The reason why I mention this is that those who believe them to have been divinely enjoined do not believe them to have been enjoined upon any except the people of Israel.

A propaganda of the Jewish Faith at this time of day would, historically speaking, resemble in some respects the propaganda which the Jew of Tarsus undertook in the first century of the Christian era. In saying this, however, I desire to be perfectly explicit. St. Paul in conducting his propaganda of the faith which was in him did not confine himself to the teaching of the Jewish religion. The age in which he lived, unlike our own, presented Judaism on the one hand, Paganism on the other. In his judgment, Theism, as he had learned it from his fathers, appeared to be incomprehensible to Greeks and Romans. He therefore taught a religious conception which differed considerably from that which he had inherited. And he himself is described as having been converted before he taught others. The only point of likeness, therefore, between the work of St. Paul and the other Jewish apostles, and that which might be done by Jews of the present generation is that the teaching of religion was then, and may again be, the work of persons who have fellowship by race with those whom the Hebrew prophets have described as the " Kingdom of Priests," the "Witness" and the " Servant." It is therefore rather in the sense of continuity in the historic mission of the people of Israel that I mention the apostles here, than for the purpose of imitating them in teaching what is subversive of the Jewish religion.

The strength of the Jewish religious position at the present time is this: It is popularly supposed that there is no other way of leading men to God than by accepting the theory of the Fall and the redemption through the death of Christ. It is imagined that, in the absence of this teaching, there is no other which is at once spiritually religious, and at the same time possessing the power and authority of long historic experience. The answer to this statement of course is the *Jewish Religion*. But the world knows nothing of the Jewish religion. Even in countries where emancipation has been accomplished for the Jews, and where society has been made acquainted with Jewish individuality or with Jewish talent in art, in jurisprudence and politics, or in finance,—the faith of the Israelite, his inner life, his life with God, the moral springs of conduct with the best of Israelites are all sealed and dead letters to the popular religious mind. The widest misapprehensions prevail as to what constitutes the actual religious faith of the best Jews and Jewesses, both in England and in America. A visit to the synagogue, which few people have made, does not throw much light on the subject, because the service and the ritual being mainly oriental in character, and not conducted in the vernacular, are scarcely intelligible to strangers. Moreover, if the service were understood, it would be found, like the Jewish pulpit utterances which *are* in English, to be largely constructed on the supposition, enforced by ages of repression, that this is a special service for a special people. The constant references to the sorrows of scattered Israel, and the number of prayers for peace to be granted " unto all Israel," deeply pathetic and obviously appropriate though they be, would not encourage the idea that Judaism is a religion for people who are not Jews. A student might with indomitable patience study for himself the history and the philosophy of the great men of Israel, and discover, after long and laborious inquiry, how much it contains which is truly universalist, and how little after all there is in it which has a merely local application. Wandering in those mines of learning in spiritual philosophy, he might be amazed, even when examining disquisitions on purely racial ordinances, how intensely human they were. He might be struck with the fact that some ritual detail symbolises a living spiritual truth of the deepest significance, with an appropriateness to the spiritual needs of men who are not Jews. In such a matter as the extraordinary minutiæ of rabbinical laws relating to the burial of the dead and the consolation of the bereaved, he might, if possessed of the necessary temperament, be astounded at the wisdom and the humanity of the intentions of the Jewish sages. Even in the cleansing of the house for Passover, he may discover a sound general proposition that in the poorest homes dust and dirt should not be permitted to accumulate beyond a definite period. In the sanitary arrangements he would doubtless be astonished at the sense and prudence, scientific as well as ethical, which are displayed in them. And in all these things he might consider that the application of such laws to masses of the Christian poor would be a godsend.

But such migrations into regions of unknown study are few and far between. My contention is this, that at the present time, amid the multitude of different movements for the promotion of the moral and intellectual progress of our species, conducted as they may be in England and America with perfect freedom, a place of worship might be opened in London by Jews with the avowed object of setting forth to those who might desire to come of their own free will, the conception of God, of worship, and of moral responsibility which the people of Israel have maintained during a period of three thousand years. Is it nothing to tell men what has been the faith even of a single group of their fellows during so vast a period? A faith which has sustained itself through the deepest human experiences of adversity, of sorrow, and of persecution—has not that faith something to testify? Is experience nothing? And what shall we say of the long, tragic, human story of love, of death, and of tribulation? Are these not the common property of mankind? What problem more catholic in its human interest than these?

And what have we to tell as the tried experience of our race as to the conception of the Deity and of the relation between God and man? Howsoever restricted may have been the earliest notions of the ancient Hebrews on this subject, owing to their inception into the first scenes of the drama of history, has not a career developed of growth, of maturity, and indeed of ripe age, from which to draw lessons of life and the story of our faith? Have we not demonstrated to the world that our religion has something about it which can survive the very conditions from which the conventional theologian would suppose it was inseparable? Passing through the successive stages of a wandering tribe, a militant theocracy, a self-governing subject race of the Roman Empire, to a spiritual communion of scattered groups of families in every quarter of the globe, and finally at this day a religious denomination in the midst of latter-day democracies, holding fast to the same aspirations, clinging to the same moral precepts, and breathing the same confession of faith in the one unseen God whom now all the Western World acknowledge through a Jewish incarnation. No people can speak of God and of faith, of prayer and of the Divine love, with greater authority and with deeper knowledge than the people of Israel. After all it must be admitted that the religious experiences of the Jewish people are, above everything, human experiences. The optimism of the Jews, without which they would long since have perished in despair, is an optimism of an intensely religious kind. Their vitality is positively the product of their religiousness. The deep-rooted belief which they have inherited consists of the idea that there is a close affinity between the human soul and the Divine Being. There is an intimacy in this relationship far closer than that existing in the mind of the ordinary Christian between himself and the Omnipresent. Less of fear and more of love forms the Jewish conception of the position of man to God. *Merciful, kind*, and *gracious*, are the Divine attributes which seem to have fastened upon the Jewish thought of God. In the second commandment, where it is said that "He visiteth the sins of the fathers upon the children," there is an overwhelming balance on the side of mercy, because that visitation is restricted to the "third and fourth generations of them that hate" God, whereas He shows "mercy to thousands of them that love Him." This is one of those ideas touching the relations of God and man which has taken hold on the Jewish mind. I refer to it only in this sense, not as any authoritative revelation, though I do not deny that it may have such signification also. The way in which Jews have to teach their message to the world is not the same as that in which the Catholic Church claims to teach. That is to say, we do not approach our neighbours with a declaration that we alone possess by mystical powers the keys of the gates of heaven; but we have a faith which is an experience, and we have to tell of our experience; in other words, we bear witness of God. The time appears to be ripe for a definite Theistic movement, and the Jews cannot be said to be the wrong people to conduct it. If there is anything in what is called revelation, the element of experience is an extraordinary corroboration. If we regard revelation, not in the miraculous sense of the Day of Pentecost, but still the discovery of essential spiritual truths, experience again is a tremendous power. If there is a revelation of God in history, in literature, and in human experience, what people can testify as a people with such force as the people of Israel? Any strong Theistic and definitely religious movement which may take place hereafter must assuredly rest its work upon foundations which cannot be shaken by the contemporaneous proceedings in the field of biblical criticism. Whatever has been shown, or remains to be proven, as to the authorship and date of the books of the Pentateuch and of the New Testament, the spiritual experience of the Jewish people stands out as something entirely independent and unmolested. What we have to testify is not of the evidence of an alleged miracle like that of the Easter morn, or, indeed, of the passage of the Red Sea; nor even of the trumpet-blowing and thick darkness on the Hill of Sinai. We speak only of a record of a vast human experience in the necessity and the efficacy of a life with God. The Israelite of to-day has as much to teach on this subject as the Jew of eighteen centuries ago. He has indeed a wider field of direct religious influence if only he has the courage and the personal gift of grace to exercise it. And here I would endeavour to indicate briefly of what kind of religion the modern Israelite may become again an apostle to the Gentiles.

Apart from the orthodox Jew's belief that he is the custodian of a written revelation intended for mankind, and already to a large extent accepted, there is the Reformed Jew, who, without fear of examining the researches of biblical critics, has his own personal faith. It is a conviction as firm and as potent at least as that of his wandering ancestors who journeyed in a wilderness. God to him is the greatest reality in human experience. The bond of human brotherhood is greater far than that of race. It is true he has no formulated creed or catechism, but herein perhaps lies his chief strength. Doctrines he certainly does hold, and theories as to the problems of sin and death he cannot shirk. There is, however, this difference between his doctrine and that of most formulated ones. He believes absolutely in the harmony—in the indissolubility—of religion and reason. At the same time he does not attempt to deny that the element of mystery is an over-mastering condition of life here and of life hereafter. The New Testament injunction that the Kingdom of Heaven opens its gates to those who become as little children is not new to him. Self-surrender and perfect humility are the conditions in which the highest spiritual truths are apprehended. Vanity and pride veil the sight from what is best. Sin is the gulf which separates the human from the divine. Sin is conquerable not by miraculous transactions, but by resolute human effort in accord with a divinely-implanted power to conquer evil. Prayer is the special privilege of human nature, by which the consciousness of the Divine Presence can be realised. It must be strictly personal, and cannot be delegated to another.

Neither is there any barrier in prayer between an individual human conscience and him who is the Father of spirits. Mediation is unknown to any Jewish conception of worship. The supreme truth about the Israelite's religion is that it is a natural religion. Individualism has a real spiritual meaning. God is revealed to each separately and distinctly, and no external or general revelation, either by miracle or otherwise, is so precious as that which may be personally felt by an effort of complete resignation in sorrow, and a strong determination in prosperity to resist the temptations of selfishness. God, who is the sovereign of perfect righteousness and of awful purity, is unutterably near to each individual soul, as if it alone existed. The relation between the Divine and human is not merely general, but is essentially personal. We become nearer, or more distant, in our relation with the Divine Being in the exact proportion of our own personal morality. Living without God and living with God are the two courses which are possible to every man and woman. And the standard of ethics or morality, however disparaging, must have reference to the ideal perfection of the infinitely righteous God. The fact that we have kinship with Him renders it possible to live a very noble life. And though we are by the finite conditions of our existence infinitesimal atoms as compared with Him, there is practically no limit to the moral possibilities for the development of human character. Whilst the mind seems abashed at the contemplation of a perfect ethical ideal in the Divine Personality, there is nothing in it to terrify or deaden human aspiration. This may perhaps be termed a mystery, but it appears to be one of the manifestations of the Divine goodness which is known by the attribute of love. There is, above all things, an unspeakable love on the part of the Infinite Creator towards His creatures. And we might, with some fitness, refer to the Hebrew Psalmist's idea that righteousness and mercy have met one another. Probably this is the most wonderful solution ever conceived of the problem of Divine perfection and human imperfection. In human experience we have the counterpart of this idea, for it is admitted that the more sinless a man is the more commiseration he has for other people. The doctrine of the love of God is no doubt the most potent of all truths which may be said to have been revealed to mankind. Of course, the human counterpart (which, generally speaking, is the parental and the filial affection) enables us to form some conception of what Divine love really means. Human affection, in its purest manifestations, sometimes between persons not united by blood, is an obvious illustration, or rather effect, of the Divine love which regulates the relations between God and humanity. A very earnest Christian has recently written a book to show that love is the greatest thing on earth. That is a truth which must be ever present in the propagation of a Theistic religion.

Such, in brief, is the character of the religious teaching which members of the House of Israel who have not separated themselves from their people might promulgate. Congregations could assemble in London and New York, composed of persons of Christian birth who are unattached to any one of the Christian communions. The time seems to have arrived when there might be an independent Theistic movement—independent in the sense that it would be neither bound by the ritual of Judaism nor be identical with Christian Unitarianism. It certainly would have sympathy with such a movement as the Theistic Church in London, founded by that able, single-minded man, the Rev. Charles Voysey; but its relations with the Old Testament and with an historic past would have the effect of bringing its adherents into a fellowship at least with the most ancient religious organisation. There are indeed important details of Jewish ritual closely knit with its deepest religious beliefs that might be recommended to and adopted by persons who are not Israelites. Even the most racial observance, the Feast of Passover, could be celebrated as the commemoration of the principle of human liberty. And those Hebrew Festivals which have their origin in the summer and autumn changes would serve as valuable landmarks in a natural religion. But with greater force could we recommend the annual day of repentance. The Day of Atonement is, above all things, connected with that alternative already mentioned in regard to the problem of sin. Without the doctrine of the Fall and miraculous redemption, sin and remission, or forgiveness of sin, must for ever confront the religious conscience. Repentance, renunciation and a reconciliation with God can never lose their claim upon the intellect as well as upon the heart of those who believe that they have relations with the one Perfect Being. The modern conception of the Day of Atonement is singularly universal in its appropriateness and in its tendency.

It is scarcely necessary to speak of that great Hebrew institution which, from its inception, was essentially applicable to the physical and moral needs of all nations, and which has been generally accepted, namely, the weekly Day of Rest and Devotion. A liturgy could be compiled on the basis of those already in use in the synagogue—translated and revised in a manner to exhibit all those elements of Judaism which are truly universal. It is scarcely necessary to add that practices which are distinctively Oriental, and not identical with the Jewish faith, would not be adopted in the plan of worship here proposed. Such matters as the covering of heads and the separation of the sexes, and the abstention from kneeling in prayer, are mere accidents of a national history, and the commonplace badges of enforced separateness. They would have no meaning for any ordinary assembly of English or American worshippers.

Such a movement as I have endeavoured most feebly and imperfectly to indicate may appear to some minds, Jewish and Christian alike, as a vague, empty dream. The question which underlies such dreams or aspirations is the question of faith and of conviction. Those who are persuaded that they are right in their conception of religion must at least desire the propagation of their views, unless it be that the conception is such as to exclude the idea that they themselves are types of other mortals. Belief and conviction, whether in science or in politics, or religion, logically involve, however, the thought of a mission. The tendency of modern and of Western civilisation is against the ancient partitioning of the human family. Whereas in former times, men seized upon what was different, and upon what could raise barriers, now we look for the means of union, of assimilation, and of broad human bonds. The separateness of the Jewish people is to the mind of the Reformed Jew not an end in itself, but a means. The long, historic isolation of Israel is to be compared with the isolation of the student or of the philosopher who is separating himself in order to equip himself for a career which is to affect others. And even the most orthodox Jew holds this doctrine, though he holds it in a manner more mystical and undefined than that in which the Reformed Jew might conceive it. The great majority of Israelites even in England would not participate in the active propagation of their faith. But such a work has always been the work of the few, not of the many. It would not, therefore, involve any serious rupture within the Jewish fold. The individuals who would engage in it should be persons who are absolutely identified with the religious communion of their fathers, and they would lose much of their spiritual influence if their preaching to the general community were to be the means of removing them from the synagogue. It may be that there are few in number among Jewish congregations who are so constituted as to render them qualified to undertake this mission. One of the most essential conditions of such a Jewish reformer must be a very high development of human sympathy. Such a qualification would stand only next to that of intense and all-absorbing faith in the religion he has to teach. In the first instance such a movement would depend primarily on the personality of those who initiated it. It sometimes happens that men are the creatures of circumstances, at other times that men appear to have been born for the age. Nothing less than the fire and the spiritual genius of a Wesley, a Baxter, or a Mendelssohn would assure the success of the first steps to the foundation of a Jewish, English, Theistic Church. On the other hand, men of less scholarship than any of these might lay the seeds of such a movement, but they must be men of no less strength of conviction and purity of purpose. Whilst the mention of such a movement may awaken the sneers of a pessimist, it is not impossible that it may be more practicable in the near future than any far-reaching reform within the Jewish body itself. And if Jewish reform were to take this direction during the present generation, it may after all be the strongest act possible to justify the claims of Higher Judaism.

REFORMED JUDAISM.

[*"Jewish Quarterly Review," January*, 1894.]

IN the fifth volume of this REVIEW I ventured to submit some suggestions upon the missionary character of Judaism in relation to those who do not belong to the Jewish race. In that essay I endeavoured to point out that the Jewish religion was one which embodied spiritual conceptions and religious beliefs of a character suitable to the religious needs of men and women beyond the confines of the race of Israel. There may be, and undoubtedly there is, some difference among Jews themselves as to the elements of Judaism which are entitled to command the first place in their own judgment, and which are of universal application. I propose, therefore, to indicate here that there is a certain mission which the House of Israel owes to itself. It is possible that the kind of Judaism which I consider capable of acceptance by non-Jews is not altogether that same Judaism which the mass of the Jewish people recognise as constituting their religion. For example, the mass of Israelites hold to a conception of worship that differs very essentially from that which alone is capable of commending itself to the Western mind, as indeed it is the only one that appeals to those who believe in the diffusion of Israel's faith.

The divergence between Jews of the present generation is a matter which cannot be ignored. For although the fundamental dogma known as the unity of God is accepted by every section of Israelites, there are distinct differences in religious conception between those who may be described as Rabbinical and as Reform Jews. Now, in using these designations, it must be understood that, however reluctant one is to do so, the necessities of language are such that it is scarcely possible to refer to different schools of thought without the use of some generic terms. The word usually employed as the antithesis of reform is "orthodox." In my view, that expression is logically objectionable in the sense in which it is used by the Jewish Community. What they actually mean by it is not simply conventionality, the sense in which the term is employed in the Anglican Church. They mean that kind of Judaism which rests entirely and exclusively upon Rabbinical authority. That is to say the Jewish religion in their view is that, and that alone, which has been defined to them by a long, series of traditions upheld and transmitted upon the authority of the Rabbis. This is nominally at least the Judaism of the vast majority of Jews in England, counting them in their corporate numbers as so many congregations. The other Judaism for which I would desire vigorous missionary efforts, and which is the only one that can be fully embraced by the modern European or American, is based upon another kind of tradition from that of

Rabbinical authority. It is the tradition of the Jewish people testifying to the experience of natural religion, and is interpreted independently of those prescriptions which constitute Rabbinical Judaism. The genius of Judaism is that it is a story of natural religion, of spiritual aspiration among individuals and families through a long series of ages. The revelation of which Rabbinism makes so much is only the tested and recorded result of spiritual experiences. But it is revelation in the supernatural and miraculous sense which stands supreme in the minds of Jews who live under the sway of Talmudical prescription. Traditional Judaism, therefore, has two distinct meanings: (*a*) The traditions of Rabbinical authority; (*b*) The spiritual experience of the Jewish race. Now, this experience is seen under different aspects, and here again we have the two distinct schools of thought which, for linguistic convenience, I have ventured to designate by the two separate terms of "Rabbinism" and "Reform." One word here as to Rabbinism. I wish it to be understood that I use that expression in no sense of disrespect. On the contrary, it represents much of the loftiest and purest features of the Jewish religion. The Rabbis as a body have been the true conservators of that very spiritual Judaism in regard to which we modern Jews have still a mission to our own race as well as a mission to the world. Tradition, and, indeed, Rabbinical tradition, has played a triumphant part in the work of transmitting to us of this age the deepest truths of ages that are passed. Rabbinism, therefore, is simply a term used here to denote that conception of Judaism which is commonly, but, I think, inaccurately termed "Orthodox." Now, the characteristic of that Judaism, which distinguishes it from the other Judaism which I desire to indicate is that it places bounds and limits to the expression of the religious idea. Another and highly important feature is that it identifies spiritual religion with ritual. The ritual of Judaism, at once historic, traditional, and possessing the majesty of fixedness, is part, and an inalienable part, of the Judaism of the Rabbinic school. The authority of the Rabbis refuses to entertain the proposition that ritualism may be severed from religion. Judaism in their view has a double aspect, both spiritual and ceremonial at the same time. A transgression against the Ritual Law is equal to a transgression against the Moral one. In fact the two are so interwoven that the ethical element is made as applicable to the one as to the other. From their standpoint they are logical in this attitude. For they maintain not merely that the Ritual Ordinances and the Moral Law proceed from the same Divine authority, but that the one is co-ordinate in importance with the other. To disobey the law of circumcision, or to eat forbidden food, or to neglect the observance of the Sabbath is, for a Jew of this type, just as sinful as it would be for an ordinary person to disregard the laws of charity, the rights of property, or the laws of chastity. This assumption of identity between two things which appear radically different to the Western mind is a tremendous demand upon the conscience—a demand so great that it is becoming more and more difficult to recognise it in the present generation. Reformed Judaism, on the other hand, recognises an inherent distinction between ritualism and spirituality. The two may be blended. They may work in harmony, and it is therefore possible for a reformer to observe all the minutiæ of traditional Judaism, but in his innermost conscience he will preserve a clear line of separation between the two. Hence Reform, in the sense in which I would fain advocate it, does not necessarily involve a violation of those ritual observances which to the old-fashioned Israelite are all important, but it does involve a mental attitude that is distinctly different from that of his so-called " orthodox " co-religionists.

Admitting, as every student of Jewish history must admit, the disciplinary value which ritualism possessed in the middle ages, one cannot be blind to the fact that it has had other consequences as well. The extraordinary detail with which ritualism pursued the life of the Israelite, and its extreme rigour, had the effect of deadening, to some extent at least, the natural impulses of the spiritual life. The office of prayer, which is the very rock of the personal religious life, has in itself sustained some injury by the excessive amount of prescription with which it was laden. A child whose earliest conception of prayer is associated with the repetition of lengthy formularies, is apt to become stunted in its spiritual growth. There is little freedom left to the human soul to cultivate its own desire to speak for itself in the Divine Presence. Multitudinous words are set down for its use in a book, and there are not many of those words which can ever become its own natural language. The essence of the religious idea is free communion with God. The shortness of life, the swiftness of time are alone sufficient to prevent the habit of free and spontaneous prayer when the set formularies are so numerous and often so incomprehensible. The habit of prayer is thus checked at the very period of life when it could best be cultivated. A very simple illustration of this spiritual drawback is the case of grace after meals. A Jewish child brought up under the old system is taught to say by rote after every meal a number of pages which it has committed to memory, instead of uttering some simple and natural expression of its gratitude to God. This illustration can be indefinitely multiplied, covering the entire range of the religious life. Any one who fully carries out the Rabbinical prescriptions as to prayer can find little opportunity for personal communion with God. This is a matter of transcendent importance, for it really covers the whole area of the spiritual life, and lies at the root of that conduct which is founded upon a religious basis. It is notorious that, whilst there are no people who say so many prayers as the "orthodox" Jews, there are none who so rarely pray. The natural prayer is not obligatory, whereas the artificial or prescribed prayer is. To the old-fashioned Israelite, worship means the reading of a book, or the recital from memory of that which he once read. He has never acquired the faculty of speaking in the Divine ear exactly what is in his heart.

There can be but little doubt that there are two distinct conceptions of the Jewish religion entertained by persons who are equally attached in loyalty and affection to their race, and who both regard Judaism as a divine message. Moreover, they both believe in the Jewish mission. They differ as to the manner of giving it effect. Between these two kinds of men there are in regard to outward observances very marked differences indeed. And such differences do in truth arise from the contrasts in their actual conceptions of the religious life. Upon the vital subject of divine worship the difference is particularly significant. That which is impressive to the one is repellent to the other. Upon the subject of the manner in which worship should be conducted, the difference of opinion and of feeling between one Jew and another is probably as wide as anything which distinguishes the Buddhist worship from that of the Greek and Latin Churches. There is scarcely, indeed, a common ground upon this particular subject. The persistent effort on the part of the

Rabbinical Jew to preserve every element of Orientalism, in utter disregard of the transformation in his own temperament, and its complete unfitness for Oriental methods, is a point upon which no compromise is possible. This Orientalism in the system of worship, however picturesque as viewed from a distance and observed by an outsider, is to a religious-minded Jew who is not of that school of thought an absolute deterrent. It is an obstacle in his path. Either it alienates him from religious communion with his brethren, or it completely destroys his faculty for worship. No one who is not a Jew can well estimate the appalling effect of the popular Jewish manner of worship upon that Jew who is not in sympathy with it. There are two distinct objects in the Rabbinical form of worship. One is, of course, the spiritual object, that of drawing men's hearts near to their Maker; and the other is to preserve intact the symbols of a remote Oriental ancestry. The combination of these two purposes seems to be a philosophical impossibility, and therefore one of them must be sacrificed to the other. Human nature is constituted in a way which renders the forms that properly belong to one age unsuitable for another. The manner in which people live and express their thoughts must necessarily vary according to the circumstances of time, place, and education. The costume, metaphorically speaking, of ancient Judæa or of the early Roman Empire is not consonant with the idiosyncrasies of later ages and of different countries. The fundamental religious beliefs may be the same, but it is humanly impossible that they can be expressed exactly in the same way. But there are still further differences besides those of mere climate and period. There are the actual contrasts arising from political and intellectual conditions. The temperament of a human being must necessarily vary when he is living as a pariah in a foreign land, afflicted by persecution, and when he is a free citizen of a State where there is no persecution. There is an unspeakable difference between the conditions of enforced separateness and those of political assimilation. The habit of life is transformed, the individual temperament is changed. To allege that the religious symbols suited to one condition are equally appropriate for another that is totally different is to attempt to do in words what cannot be done in reason. The experiment is doomed to failure. And the experience of the present century in England—the only period when the matter can be said to have been fairly tested—proves that the loss to the cause of spiritual religion is greater than the gain to that of external racial continuity.

The alteration in the manner of public worship which has been effected among the English Jews in the present century is almost infinitesimal. Substantially they worship in the same manner as their ancestors did a thousand years ago, and as their brethren do in the present day throughout Russia and Poland. There is no correspondence whatever in the change of their ritual observances with the other changes that have come over every other department of their lives. Neither is there any prospect that within the lines of Rabbinical Judaism an organic change will take place. A change not less than that which distinguishes the Oriental from the Occidental is the aim of that reform which I would advocate; and such a change would not be regarded as permissible by any Rabbinical authority as at present constituted. What, then, is the future of Judaism? Historical continuity, no doubt, is assured; identity of forms and ceremonies is guaranteed; but what of spiritual expansion within these restrictions? What of the real message of religion so carefully treasured by countless generations? Can English and American Jews be sure that their descendants will be able to receive that message through a medium which is growing less and less serviceable to each successive generation? This is the problem for the present generation of English-speaking Jews and Jewesses. Can we pretend that the outward forms of religion have the same attribute of eternity which belong to those divine truths which they are said to represent? Is not the idea of eternity, or at least of unalterableness, the special and exclusive attribute of what is abstract? In dealing with this question it seems necessary to refer briefly to the common opinion that outward forms are of little or no consequence. By a strange paradox, this is the answer put forth by Rabbinical Jews to those who now desire organic changes in the ritual. But in reality, these very people hold forms to be of so much consequence that they will not yield even to the bitter cry that such observances fail to appeal to the present generation. It is, however, a broad truth of singular import, that outward forms are not casual and trifling things. They profoundly affect the inner springs of religion, both on its spiritual and its moral sides.

In ordinary affairs, outside the sphere of religion, external forms are of so much consequence that many are unable to digest food which is perfectly healthy unless it is prepared and served in a particular way. There is no greater popular fallacy than the cry that external manners and outward things are of little consequence. Numerous illustrations could be cited to show that, in various stages of civilisation which represent different conditions of men and women, such matters are in reality quite vital. In religion, more than in most things, outward forms constitute all the difference which distinguishes the natural temperaments of one group of people from another. This accounts for the fact that Christianity, which is fundamentally the same, so far as the central doctrine of the resurrection of Christ is concerned, to every Christian in Europe, yet presents the extraordinary varieties which may be instanced by the mention of the Roman Catholic Church and of the Salvation Army. As to doctrine, the differences are as nothing compared with their concurrence upon the questions of the Incarnation, the Atonement, and the Resurrection. They differ largely as to externals and to discipline. And yet, if it were not possible to be a Christian except upon the terms of the Salvation Army, or upon those of the Church of Rome, Christendom would be enormously diminished. The same truth is even more applicable to the Jewish religion. Even if such a Reform Judaism as I desire were in existence, its differences from Rabbinic or traditional Judaism would be mainly in the sphere of outward forms, and only slightly in that of Dogma. There would inevitably be a striking contrast between a Rabbinic synagogue and a Reformed one; but the faith would be practically identical. The position of Rabbinic Judaism, on the other hand, is this :—You can only belong to the Jewish religion on certain terms. Here comes the need for that revolution which the present generation of emancipated Jews is called upon to institute. We claim to profess the same faith as the author of the 143rd Psalm. We desire that same free communion with the Eternal Spirit which the Israelite who composed that Psalm enjoyed. We claim to hold that communion in our own way, and not according to prescription. I know I shall be told that such a claim will be the forerunner of many sects within Judaism. And here it is necessary to speak of sects.

There was a time in every country when there was an intolerance of sect, and when uniformity was the watchword. The word uniformity has lost its charm and the word sect has lost its sting. The fundamental dogmas of Judaism are of such incomparable breadth, and the racial tie of Israel is so incalculably strong, that even the multiplication of religious sects within Israel's fold presents no cause for disruption or alarm. We have reached a stage in the history of Judaism, and in the history of our race, when there is room, ample and abundant, for varied expressions of those Hebrew truths which are eternal. But this fear of sects becoming numerous is misplaced. For from the very nature of the case they could not number more than they do at present. We already possess the two distinct rituals or Minhagim of the Sephardim and the Ashkenazim, with their different Hebrew pronunciations, and their separate organisation and government in the same town. Then come the Reform synagogues, already established in England, America, and Germany, of which scarcely two are exactly alike. These reforms, so far as England is concerned, have been what I would respectfully describe as timid and tinkering. Not one of them has effected that organic change in the externals of public worship which is so urgently required. There should be a definite change in our attitude towards those forms which have no justification in the present age, except that they are traditional. I freely admit the powerful claim which that word tradition has upon the intellectual judgment of every thoughtful person. But what I contend is that the tradition of the spiritual religion of Judaism is being sacrificed for the tradition of its mediæval customs. The shell of Judaism is being studiously preserved, while the religion of the Hebrew prophets and psalmists is becoming obscured. The revision of the Prayer Book is of vital consequence. The prayers require to be reset and recast, in order to express at once the historical continuity of Israel and the religious thoughts of people of our own time. It is surely incongruous that the prayer which is offered in a London synagogue for the Queen and her Government should be expressed in precisely the same words that are used in Russia for the Czar and his rule. If they are appropriate in the one case, they must be inappropriate in the other.

It would appear that the reason for the strong opposition to reform is due to the obscuration of the supreme elements of the Jewish religion. And what are these elements? Do they begin and end with the unity of God? Surely not! The people of Israel have transmitted a religion which I believe is adaptable to persons of every race and clime. It certainly includes faith in the Universal Father of the spirits of all flesh. And that faith is free from the terrors of a God of wrath, of an angry Deity, of a God who has accursed His own children, and made it necessary to ransom them afresh. The Hebrew conception of God,—knowing no need of mediation, holding forth free access for the human conscience to its Creator,—is this not a message of inestimable bounty to the world at large? The question arises, Do Jews themselves comprehend what it is which the religious genius of their race has revealed to mankind? Judaism freed from its racial padlocks, becomes transformed into a religion at once limitless in its application and divine in its essence. Christianity in its earlier history did but faintly translate to a pagan world the inspiration of its Hebrew founders. Christianity is itself an earnest of a world-wide Theism, and of a kingdom of heaven which is within. Judaism in its ultimate expansion—not in the Churches founded at Calvary, but in the wider and more Catholic Church founded out of a fresh reform within the Synagogue itself—is nothing short of a message to mankind betokening the love of a universal God and the brotherhood of the human race. Bursting the bounds of locality and the limits of a family tradition, it is destined to become the religion of a larger humanity than any which is at present embraced either within the Western or the Eastern Churches of Christendom. Judaism, with its independence of the crushing dogma of the Fall and of the normal perdition of the human soul; Judaism, with its glowing optimism of free salvation to all human beings, with its consecrated fire of passionate devotion to a Being without form or shape, and with its fervid love of a tender Deity who is merciful and long-suffering, has without doubt a future of statelier and of more soul-stirring magnitude than any religion which the history of the world has produced. The justification of long ages of separation, sometimes enforced from without, not infrequently established from within, will become manifest in the sight of those very people who have wailed and prayed over a so-called Christ-rejecting people. Continuity will be established between one era in the history of this world-famed ancestral faith and another. The work of the Apostles in the first century of the Christian era will come to be regarded as an instalment of the Hebrew message to the world. Christianity, in its later and broader developments will carry with it so many tokens, one by one, of the simpler and sublimer Theism of which it is only the preparation.

All this progress and advance depends upon the Jews themselves, upon those who are emancipated. It rests with us to elect between archæology and religion. The problem forces itself upon modern Jews here in England whether they will be content to keep their treasure locked up in dusty safes, and hidden from the view of mankind, or make it known and spread it broadcast.

The whole of this problem resolves itself into the question of reform. Do the Jews themselves rightly understand what it is they have suffered for through the ages? Have they themselves a right conception of the faith which is in them? Are the

Jewish people, as a body, conscious of the fact that their religion is essentially a universal religion, and that it is one which is specially capable of satisfying the natural cravings of the human soul? It is doubtful whether these facts have been realised. It is more than probable that under the dominion of Rabbinical prescription, the ordinary view entertained by Jews and Jewesses of their religion is that it is entirely a family religion, and one not designed for the spiritual requirements of other people. It is not brought home to the conscience of the Jewish community that their fondest prayers are those in which every religious nature in Christendom delights. The very fact that every nation of Christendom has unreservedly taken into its own language the prayers and hymns of the Jewish psalmists is a conclusive proof that Judaism, as expounded in those Psalms, is the religion of a much larger world than the people of Israel. Such a Psalm as the 143rd, to which I have already alluded, and a number of others, show that the religious genius of Israel has touched the keynote of the universal religious consciousness. The 51st Psalm is one more among many illustrations. Again, the 103rd, the 139th, and the 90th Psalms all reveal spiritual experiences which are neither national nor communal, because they are unspeakably human. It has never been suggested that compositions of this character have not proceeded out of the inmost sanctuary of the Jewish religion. Nor are we aware that either

Greek or Roman has bequeathed to the Western World anything precisely of this nature. The real verities of Judaism are just those thoughts and aspirations to which Psalms like these give utterance, not its ritual or its Rabbinical observances. The soul to which that wonderful verse in the 143rd Psalm is a reality, namely, " Teach me to do thy will ; . . . . . thy spirit is good ; lead me into the land of uprightness "—that soul has grasped the substance of spiritual religion which can never be bettered either by the most elaborate ritual or the most complex metaphysical creed. No religious voice in Europe could ever venture to dispute this proposition. Many have sought to fit into those words, and into others like them, some creed which was not in the mind of the person who first conceived them. But what we may claim for Judaism is that the thoughts, the strivings of every devout soul, are just those thoughts and those strivings which constitute the substance of the Hebrew Faith. A God, who is the perfection of love as well as the perfection of knowledge, is the highest Being who has ever been conceived. No race and no Church have contemplated a Deity with attributes more universal than these. It was a retrogression on the part of Paul when he stooped to represent God with human passions, requiring a compromise between the demands of His justice and the demands of His mercy. Paul, I would venture to submit, had not fully grasped the highest ideal of

Deity as we find it in such Psalms as those I have mentioned, and in the Jewish Liturgy of a later date. We have in the New Testament and the Apocrypha other instances of the intensity with which individual Israelites had apprehended the Divine Being. "In my Father's house are many mansions," and "Inasmuch as ye do it to the least of these ye do it unto me," and "Pray to thy Father which is in secret," are all so many fragments of religious genius, which abundantly testify to the universality of the religious idea as conceived by the spokesmen of the Jewish race. With his usual picturesque exaggeration the late Lord Beaconsfield observed in his life of Lord George Bentick that "No one ever wrote under the inspiration of the holy spirit except a Jew." There was development, however, in those writings, and one Jew excelled another time after time in his wider conception of a Universal God. More than one Rabbi of the Middle Ages has excelled some of the Apostles in his conception of God. But none of them have surpassed, if any have reached, the spiritual heights which were attained by the unknown Hebrew who composed the 139th Psalm. Here we have the story of the individual soul, stripped of nationality and caste, in its personal and secret relations with the Divine Being. Here is likeness to God. Here is affinity between the created and immortal soul on the one hand, and the eternal Divine Fountain of Love on the other. In connection with such language terms like those of "Jew" and "Gentile" shrink into nothingness, and we have before us the abstract human and the abstract Divine singularly blended into a harmony, which can only be likened to that of mother and child. The tenderness and catholicity of this Psalm unmask the false theory that, up till the Christian era, Judaism conceived a God of vengeance and a tribal God. If, in the age of Christ, reform within the Jewish community had been possible, a very different religious history would have followed from that which has disfigured the face of Europe for a thousand years and more. Still, in spite of the compromise of the first of those centuries, the spiritual genius of the House of Israel has slowly penetrated the Western mind. In every translation of the Hebrew Scriptures, as well as in their use in the New Testament, we perceive the message of Judaism to mankind. At the present time we find in England a true religious bond between the educated Christian and the educated Jew. There is scarcely any difference at all between the Christian Theist and the Reformed Jew. If Jews and Christians would each in their turn recognise this bond, and seek to cultivate it, a new era would be initiated in the religious history of mankind.

The special object of this essay is to place before my own brethren in race and creed the paramount claims of that kind of reform which seems essential to the furtherance of Israel's mission. We stand in need at the present moment of a loosening of the tie which has so long bound the ritual of one particular age to the changing religious sentiments of all subsequent ages, a tie which tends to suffocate those religious sentiments with the strings of an antique but outworn ritual. We require to adapt our eternal faith to the changed temperament and the altered education of new generations. The future triumph of Judaism can never be thwarted, but it may be delayed by a want of proportion in our estimate of the relation in which an historic ritual stands to permanent truths. So long as we permit our youth to discover that the first kindling of the religious flame within them takes place in a Christian place of worship and not in a Jewish one, we are retarding the progress of our Mission. There is every reason why this grave difficulty, so loosely and lightly estimated by the general community of Jews, should speedily be obviated. When we have removed this one obstacle, then, indeed, will Jews and Christians be able to unite in the utterances of those striking words: "Mine eyes have seen thy salvation, which shall be a light to lighten the Gentiles, and to be the glory of thy people Israel."

THE UNIVERSAL ELEMENT IN JUDAISM.*

IN complying with the request of the Editor of this publication to write an article for its anniversary number upon the "Universal element in Judaism," I ask myself the question—What is that element in any religious system which can be said to be universal? It is something which is free from the tints of separateness, independent of any mark that would be distinctive of nationality, race, or tribe. In other words, it must be that which is specially human, an idea or a belief or a group of thoughts which appeal straightway to human nature, irrespective of such idiosyncrasies or moods as betoken the limits of locality. What is that in Judaism which answers to this description? Some persons would deny, blindly I think, that Judaism incorporates anything which is not of the nature of a caste religion. The misconception and ignorance about the Jewish religion is one of the astounding facts of modern times. The supposition that because the Jewish race has been separate and

---

* This essay appeared in the anniversary number of the *Lyceum Weekly of Keneseth Israel*, Philadelphia, U.S.A., 1894.

distinct for three thousand years, there is nothing which is universal in its religion, represents the low-water mark of ignorance and misconception in regard to the subject.

The separateness or the distinctiveness of the Jewish people and the universality of the religion which they are preserving are two facts that are supposed to be incongruous. The incongruity, however, is only apparent, and by no means real. In truth, there is nothing incongruous in the case; on the contrary, viewed in a broad philosophic light, the separateness of the Jewish people is nothing but a means to an end, the end being the ultimate propagation of something which they have preserved by keeping themselves apart, namely their religion.

Most religious systems of the world hang upon the name of some special individual, either historic or fictional, who is identified with a particular soil. This, probably, is the case with the religions of India, China, and those of the ruder populations of Africa. Even Mohammedanism, despite its inherent doctrine of monotheism, is fastened to a name. Christianity itself is identified with a certain personality who is almost incomprehensible to those races who have not derived their civilisation either from Greece or Palestine. The Jewish religion, however, is not fastened to any name, in the same sense, beyond the fact that its sacred books are the products of particular authors, and that one author would take precedence of another in the degree of the importance of his writings, or, if you will, of his inspiration. The religion itself, that which these authors expounded or revealed, touches the universal conscience of mankind, inasmuch as it postulates the relation of the human soul with the universal and incorporeal Deity. It is the conception of God first and foremost which invests Judaism with the characteristics of a Universal Religion. The God of the Hebrew Bible and of the later Jewish writings, the God of the New Testament, and the God of the Koran is the same Being, the difference relating only to the manner of His manifestation to mankind and not in regard to His essence.

The development of the religious idea within the fold of Israel traced in the successive parts of Scripture, in mediæval Rabbinism, and in latter-day reform movements, testifies to the truth that the apprehension of the Divine Being among the Jews rises and broadens ever in the same direction, namely, that of a God who is the Father of the spirits of all flesh. The Jewish conception of prayer, and indeed the historic Jewish prayers themselves, bear witness that this people seem to hold the key which can unlock the universal religion of mankind.

Even the ritual of Judaism, with all its characteristics of local colour and family tradition, bears the impress of catholicity, for it lifts into the service of its rites sentiments which are not merely common to all men and to every part of the world, but which are specially indicative of those wants and those aspirations which cannot be said to be peculiar to only one group of human beings. The two cardinal details of Jewish Ritual are without doubt the observance of the Sabbath and that of the Passover. In both cases the keynotes are two human needs of universal application, namely, rest, and liberty. In neither case is the celebration commemorative of any personage either historical or fictional, but mainly of an abstract principle, and the principle in each case is essentially human and therefore universal.

The first difficulty which presents itself in the discussion of a great question, and especially of a religious one, is the different senses in which the same words are used. And here it must be observed that people are not agreed as to the definition of such terms as *Judaism—religion—*and *universal.* In writing about them, therefore, it seems desirable that I should briefly state my own definitions of them.

By *Judaism*, I mean the apprehension of the religious idea which the Jewish people has possessed and developed from its earliest history to the present time.

By *religion* I mean that embodiment of ideas which lies at the root and which fulfils the aspirations of human character.

The term *universal* denotes that kind of embodiment which seems appropriate for mankind at large, as distinguished from other embodiments which are confined to the peculiarities of particular groups of men and women.

Where, then, it may be asked, can we find any authoritative statement of what does constitute the religious idea which the Jewish people has possessed and developed from its earliest history to the present time? The answer seems far to seek. I, for one, would submit, however, that we gather the religious ideas of a people from their writings and from the example of their chief exponents first; and secondly, we gather it from the characteristics which have distinguished them from other peoples.

In regard to the religious idea, the chief characteristic of the Jewish people in all ages has been its abiding trust in an unseen God. The writings of its greatest exponents reveal the nature of that trust and the nature of that God whom it conceives.

The apprehension of a Supreme Being behind nature, through nature, and above nature is a thought to which every race in the history of mankind has laid some claim. There is no people of antiquity, whatever their degree of civilisation, who have not had some share in the impulse to worship something outside of themselves. The faculty of worship is, therefore, a human faculty common to all peoples, just as much as those physical faculties without which no human being ever existed. It may be said that it is impossible to find any one religious system which is suitable to every people and to all individuals. And here we are not far from the truth. Inasmuch as human character is so variable, and that no two persons are exactly alike, no one system, in the sense of an organised method, can be universally appropriate. Hence it is that the use of the term universal has its limits, its qualifications. And we are driven, when referring to a subject which involves social conditions, to use such a word as universal in a restricted philosophical sense. It would be true to say that water satisfies a universal need, that it has a use for every type of human being, and that no people can exist without it. In the realm of abstract thought, however, there is possibly nothing of which it can be said, "No human being can exist without this." On the other hand, there are moods and impulses common to the whole human species, that is to say, there are certain attributes which may be found in every type of humanity. The word universal applied to such attributes, or to the ideas which seem to fit into them, is, therefore, a philosophical rather than a physical term. It represents something which is human in the widest possible sense. Is there any kind of religion which we can conceive as being fitting to the moods and impulses of all mankind? "No, certainly not," is the inevitable reply. An Aboriginal cannibal cannot possibly share the same spiritual or intellectual experiences with a high-bred European or Asiatic. He has neither the capacity nor the need. Consequently it would be inaccurate to say of any religious idea that it is universal in the same sense in which we can say that water and air are universal. It must be remembered that philosophy borrows the use of terms which properly only belong to the physical world, and this is one of them. A universal idea in religion is something which is capable of fitting with the religious capacities of persons of different race and climate. It is on this account that Christianity in some of its aspects has established its claim to be a universal religion. The existence of an Armenian Church and of an English one are evidences that under varied conditions the doctrines which they hold in common are applicable to very different peoples. Judaism has not yet had the opportunity or the means of proving that it is capable of becoming the religion of different races. And here is the crux of the question. My contention is that the only reason why Judaism has not so demonstrated its claim to universality is because it has been artificially compressed and enclosed within the limits of a single race. But so tremendous is its inherent quality of catholicity that, in spite of the artificial padlocks which have enclosed it, it has, by the natural law of survival of the fittest, burst the padlock, and its ideas—some of its loftiest conceptions—have poured themselves out in all directions, and filled to overflowing the vessels of so-called alien creeds. All that is spiritual in the religion of Islam is the Monotheism of the Hebrew race. And when we come to consider Christianity, it is enough to say that its strange conception of a Deity manifesting Himself in the flesh, and presenting to mankind the ideal human character, is an incarnation which took the form of a typical Hebrew, who from first to last identified himself with the idealisation of the Jewish Religion. The fact that such a representation has appealed to so many millions of persons of different race and locality is in itself an overwhelming *primâ facie* evidence that Judaism must have contained within itself religious conceptions which are universal. Buddhism has not spread in the West, in anything like the volume with which this other Eastern religion has done. Large as its following is, it is essentially confined to particular regions of the earth, and to certain types of Oriental people. The circumstance on the other hand that the life and character of a particular Asiatic Jew could spread a magnetic influence, reaching, after a lapse of centuries, to the Western Hemisphere, having already covered the face of Europe, is one the significance of which is of immense consequence to this argument. So far then has the universal element of Judaism manifested itself from out of a casket which has been artificially enclosed and even enveloped. There is yet another fact about Judaism akin to this one, which proves that it has universality, namely, the marvellous adaptability of the Jewish race itself. Whilst Judaism has not been proclaimed as the national religion of England,

France, America, Jews have become Englishmen, Frenchmen, Americans. Their religion has not only not disqualified them for practical assimilation with every nationality in the world, but it has in my view been the cause and the reason why they have been more capable than any other race of such assimilation. Because their Religion had universal elements, because it was so human and so free from taints of caste and tribalism, have they been trained and educated to form part of every other nation. Their religion has been the source of whatever was great about them; and the religion of their ancestors has been the qualification by which through the law of heredity they have been able to fulfil the unparalleled achievement of uniting their racial religion with the life and duties of diverse citizenship. This could not have been accomplished if the Jewish religion had not contained within itself the elements of a universal religion. And it is just because it has so contained them that we have this remarkable result.

What then is this element of Judaism that is universal?

Writing from the inner circle of Jewish ideas, I feel rather disposed to ask myself the question, What after all is that element in Judaism which is *not* universal? For to my own mind—and in a matter of this nature a Jew can best record his personal conviction — the elements of Judaism which are not universal, that is to say, which are purely racial, are those only that serve the purpose of identifying us as the one people on earth who have apprehended the religion of mankind. The ceremonial of Judaism, and only here in part, contains elements of a distinctive character partaking of family tradition. Such, for instance as the obligation upon an Israelite to preserve the knowledge of the Hebrew language. A further duty of the Israelite is to maintain an unbroken record of his religious past and to commemorate it. These things certainly are elements of a non-universal kind. They apply only to the Jews, and would lose their import if they were converted into any other use. But these, I contend, are but the sign manual, the badges of stewardship—they do not constitute the religion of Israel; they do not compose that spiritual life which it has been the mission of the Israelite to make known to the world. Therefore to appreciate what it is in Judaism which is universal, one must pass through the curtain of Orientalism, remove the veil of family life, and enter into the inner sanctuary of Jewish Faith. The conception of God as the Creator and King of the Universe, combining the parental relation to every human being, is the most complete universalism which a religious idea can embody. Then comes the fact that the salvation of the human soul is not dependent either upon belief or selection. Its perdition, indeed, has never been suggested by Judaism, and is altogether an imagination foreign to, and absolutely at variance with, the teachings of Judaism. What religion is so universal as this?

Salvation by faith—which necessarily means a particular faith—is unquestionably a less universal conception than one which raises no theological difficulty whatever to the question of peace after death. Salvation by faith is, on the other hand, a less universal religion for the very reason that it involves a particular faith. The subject of Catholicity in regard to a Religion is approached by many religions with totally different conceptions of universalism. The Cross and the Crescent claim a universality because they demand that by them alone each for each is the salvation of the human soul possible; whereas Judaism makes no such claim just because its conception of God is so transcendentally catholic that it believes Him to be infinitely near to every human soul as if it alone existed, and that He imposes no such conditions of salvation as are taught by other conceptions. From the Jewish point of view the love of God is universal, and is not coloured by any such conflict between His justice and His mercy as, for example, the dominant Christian creed presumes.

Again, the absence of the doctrine of the Fall is in itself an assurance that Judaism is more fit for a universal religion than if it contained that dogma; for the fall of man is based upon the record of an individual act, the individual, if he ever existed, having been one of whom there could be no cognisance on the part of races who never heard of him or of any fiction relating to him. For this reason, Christianity is much less a universal religion than Judaism. Its fundamental conception of Adam's sin is incomprehensible to persons who could have no acquaintance with the literature in which the name of Adam appears. The Hindus, the Chinese, and the races of Africa, who are not Mohammedans, cannot possess any consciousness or suspicion of having been descended from Adam. The spread of Christianity amongst such people is, therefore, confronted at the outset with the palpable injustice of being held to bear the hereditary guilt of one from whom they cannot even imagine themselves to have sprung. The enormous importance, both logically and structurally, which this idea of Adam and his sin holds in the Christian hypothesis of God's relation to mankind, is apt to be overlooked. If there was no first man, and if there was no hereditary guilt attaching to his sin, the ransom, and the atonement, and the resurrection of Christianity must find some other basis. Judaism, it is true, has its folk-lore and its legends about a first man and even a first man's sin—this identical Adam—all of which some Jews accept literally and some do not. But in either case the story has not been used by Judaism to found a dogma upon which its entire religion is built up, as is the case in Christianity. Judaism merely reveals the conception of an Infinite Deity, who, though selecting the people of Israel for a special purpose, is essentially the God and the Father of all peoples. The most important documents of the Jewish religion deal mainly with this conception of God; and of His special dealings with Israel, the references are secondary to those of His dealings with mankind. In almost every case Israel is spoken of as a means to an end, a "servant," a "messenger," or a "Kingdom of Priests"; but God and humanity form the real subject of the theme, the ultimate aim of the writing.

It must be admitted that the Psalms and the writings of the Hebrew prophets are the most authoritative expressions of Hebrew faith. Who that has ever heard of them can do without them if he needs a religious inspiration? If they were entirely racial and particularist in character and scope, they could not possibly serve the use which they already fulfil in so many religions outside Judaism. Is there any other religion whose sacred literature is thus employed among the followers of different creeds? What stronger evidence could be adduced that Judaism contains that which is universal? Christianity, with all its differences from Judaism in regard to the theory of sin and redemption, and even touching the definition of the word Unity, has found itself forced not only to use the most authoritative literature of the Jewish race in the sense in which a cultivated European uses Greek literature, but it positively claims for it that it embodies the word of God revealed through Judaism and Christianity at once to mankind. This is a tremendous testimony to the universalism inherent in the Jewish religion. The Hebrew Bible, written in the East by a special people, amid every circumstance of an antique Orientalism, is yet found after the lapse of ages to contain thoughts and ideas and experiences which are fundamentally applicable to the requirements of Western civilisation, and to the advanced political ideas of the United States of America. Anybody who could say, in the face of this fact, that Judaism has not an element of universality, must be blindly ignorant. And yet, amid all the changes of ages, these same writings hold the same vital place in Judaism, which they did before the knowledge of them was extended.

It might be supposed that no two religions could be more diverse than Judaism and Christianity. And in regard to some vital problems this is true. 1. The possibility of God taking upon himself human nature is contrary to the Jewish idea of a Deity who is essentially incorporeal. 2. The assumption that any conflict could arise in the mind of God between His different moral attributes, such as His justice and His mercy, is opposed to the Jewish view of God's infinite and incomprehensible perfection. 3. And last, but not least, the logical difficulty of a Triunity in Unity has no trace whatever in the documents of Judaism, and does not appeal to the Jewish understanding. With these differences, which cannot be minimised, Judaism has yet been able to be of incalculable service to Christianity, both in its origin and subsequent development. The New Testament is not merely impregnated with the Old, but Christians of every type assure us that it would have been inconceivable without it. Such, then, is the almost miraculous part which Judaism has played in religions which so widely differ from it, that it might have been imagined that the one could not have entered into the other. If, then, Judaism can do so much for races who have adopted Christianity, why shall it not be of equal and of greater service to other races who have hitherto adopted no distinctive theology? Nothing but a pure human element, mystical by reason of its intensity, and, therefore, divine, could account for the spiritual and widely diffused power already manifested by Judaism. So much has been done in spite of enclosing, suppressing, and restricting. What if Judaism be boldly proclaimed to the world without let or hindrance?

THE DAY OF MEMORIAL.

*[Reprinted from the " Jewish Chronicle,"
September 27th, 1889.]*

ONE of the most striking features in Judaism is its singular power of adaptability. By adaptability we mean appropriateness—something which meets the needs of all men. It is not surprising that Judaism possesses this feature, for if it did not it is inconceivable how it could have lasted over such a vast span of time; how so many generations of the race, differently situated and under so many varying conditions, could have adhered to it, and do adhere to it still. Judaism contains within its system and organisation, a grasp of moral perceptions and a conception of life generally which must sooner or later attract the most diverse people, embracing as they do the moral and spiritual conditions of human character. This is our title to be considered a race endowed with the gift of Universality. Strange enough just the people who are popularly but ignorantly supposed to be the most separate and exclusive are they who possess in the most marked degree a Religion suited to all mankind. Indeed, the fact may be stated with greater emphasis. That one people which is so distinct is so, just because it is the one people charged with the preservation of a religion that is capable of becoming Universal. The present season suggests a powerful illustration of this argument. There is probably no man, woman or child in England, Christian or otherwise, who would not be the better for observing the Day of Memorial; that is to say, the general conception of that institution which gathers round it the entire circle of thought, taking account of the moral imperfections as well as the moral possibilities of human nature, is one that might be taught with the most excellent consequences to all kinds of people beyond the limits of the Jewish Race. The Day of Memorial, like the Day of Atonement, is not the anniversary of any historical occurrence of specially racial interest, such as the Passover or even the Pentecost. It is simply an historic record in the Hebrew Calendar that Judaism has, from its commencement, appropriated the chief season of the year for the purpose of making a special effort annually to consider a question of vital issue to all men, namely the question of personal moral and spiritual regeneration.

There is no doubt that, even with Jews themselves, the Day of Memorial and the Day of Atonement mean very different things, more or less associated with family tradition and with ritual. But to state the case in anything like a comprehensive manner, it is necessary to insist that the recurrence of these days in the Jewish Calendar means nothing less than the recurrence of the problem, " What shall we do to make ourselves better before God and our own consciences." It is this endeavour, repeated every year, which in an individual and in the history of a people is calculated to produce very important results in the moral aspect of human life. The Day of Memorial means the day of calling to remembrance, the day on which a probing of the heart and conscience is to take place preparatory to the day on which, having discovered the actual failings in personal conduct, repentance takes place, accompanied with renewed hopes. The calling to remembrance or the probing of one's personal moral condition is a proceeding which Judaism recommends to or enforces upon every individual, however divergent one may be from another in his moral and spiritual condition at the time. Some meet this day literally laden with sin; others meet it if not so laden, yet conscious of much imperfection. And the exact measure of the particular condition is, according to Judaism, referred not to any human or popular standard of right and wrong, but solely to the claims of perfect righteousness. We gather this from the emphasis with which all Hebrew religious teaching impresses on us the essential affinity between man and God, and of the close and constant tie which connects the human and divine. A people chosen of God, just that one nation of antiquity who thought about righteousness, may very properly be regarded as the correct type or illustration of the sort of bond which should be consciously recognised between every human soul and its Creator. The Supreme Being, whose main attributes are those of perfect righteousness, is then the Ideal as well as the Judge of human conduct. This, no doubt, is a very severe test, far more overwhelming indeed than any which could be supplied from what is known as the requirements of public opinion or the customs of a particular society. But whilst it is overwhelming in the magnitude of its claim it is also more compassionate by far than any judgment instituted by social custom. Almighty God is the Father and Friend, as well as the Judge of Mankind. By reason of His own perfect righteousness are we better able to approach Him—even when laden with sin—than we should be able to meet a human friend who is only partially righteous.

One naturally reflects on the balance of attributes even in the Divine Being, and the first thing which strikes the observation amid such reflections is that idea which Judaism pronounces with incomparable force, namely, the infinite love of God. God loves His creatures, we are told; He takes pleasure in their righteousness as well as commanding it. If we may so speak, after the manner of the Hebrew prophets, God takes a delight in our desire to become righteous. "He takes no pleasure in the death of the wicked, but rather that he may turn from his wicked ways and live." Just as the standard of right and wrong is a higher one in the light of man's relation to God, so the means of turning towards righteousness or seeking a perfect ideal is infinitely more attractive and therefore easier than seeking merely to satisfy a popular notion of right. Popular notions are always variable. The Divine standard does not vary. Then again popular notions and public opinion take account only of acts or of thoughts which present an immediate external expression, and they care not at all about motives. Whereas with the Divine Judgment the reverse is the case. It is possible that in the sight of God many men and women whom society counts among the worthy are just where others are whom society condemns. People whom the world regards with favour may be in the sight of God and in reality quite corrupt. The genius of Judaism is nowhere better displayed than in this matter of repentance and regeneration. The whole proceeding is an affair between the individual and God himself. What the Jewish preacher or homilist has to do on a day like the Day of Memorial is, simply to remind his hearers that this is the occasion on which Judaism prompts a man to probe his conscience and to analyse the actions of his past life. But nobody wants to know the result, and no good can come of one person venturing to form a judgment on the conduct of another.

At this season all Israel halts, not to take counsel with one another, but each with his God.

Nothing is proposed of the nature of sacerdotalism or confession one to another. No reparation for sin can be accomplished by any ritual transaction whatever. It is an act of introspection, solemnised by being conducted in connection with the worship of God. No institution is better calculated to stimulate the virtue of charity. The Day of Memorial and the Day of Atonement are probably times of all others when the average Israelite would be least disposed to say anything harsh about his neighbour. For whatever be the degrees of virtue or sin in each person, greater prominence is given to one's own imperfections than to any other consideration. In fact, it is with that matter, and that alone, with which the Israelite is concerned on these days. Anybody who is more or less satisfied with his personal moral state on any particular Day of Atonement is likely to be either appalled at the discovery of much sin in himself, or if he finds that he is a person whose temptations have been few and whose general preference has been to pursue a right course rather than a wrong one, he must be all the more absorbed with the sense of being still so far from the great Ideal, that he has been able to keep more frequently present than other persons. Again, a self-examination—if it be a true one—must be found to depend largely upon taking account of facts which are really known only to oneself, and the very process illustrates how vain it is to judge correctly about other people, of whom the most important details can be known only by themselves. So that either way the common vice of uncharitably judging one's neighbour receives a positive check and is practically suppressed on these occasions. What is proposed to be done on those days is something which excludes for the time the ordinary forces of public opinion. It is a time when public opinion is not referred to, but rather put out of sight; and we are brought face to face with that kind of tribunal in which the obvious course is to be absolutely confidential. Nobody is really present at what goes on between a human conscience and God, save the individual concerned. There is no inducement to be evasive or to attempt to hide any fact from the One Omniscient. Complete frankness is what would naturally prompt anybody in such circumstances, alike in his introspection and in his communion with God.

Thus the universality of Judaism has been shown by its peculiar consideration of those conditions in the moral sphere which are common to all mankind. But the institution of the Day of Memorial, and the manner of its observance, further indicate in another direction the idea of universality. Any one who examines the Jewish Liturgy appointed for the Day of Memorial must be struck with the special prominence there given to those attributes of the Supreme Being which suggest His common Fatherhood and the common brotherhood of His creatures. Throughout those pages we read much less of the "Guardian of

Israel" than we do of the "Creator of all worlds," and the "Father of all men." That distinctness of race which naturally finds expression in Jewish public worship on many occasions seems to be put aside by the influence of the Day of Memorial. The "New Year's Day" as it is called (whatever may be thought of it as an historical pretension), lays claim to celebrate the stupendous fact that "In the beginning God created the heavens and the earth," and that "He created man in His own image." This notion is quite independent of any assumption about the manner or the date of creation. No student of Biblical criticism will suffer his critical faculty to be disturbed by recognising that this particular Day of Memorial is celebrated for the 5650th time. The religious and philosophical import of such a celebration neither loses nor gains by importing into it or rejecting from it assertions to the effect that the world is so many years old. That is a matter apart from what is here considered. The reckoning of time in Christendom and in Mohammedanism is arranged with reference to events which signify the birth of the founder of the particular religion. It might have been so with Judaism. The birth of Moses or the Exodus from Egypt, or the building of the first Temple, could conceivably have served the purpose of dating the Hebrew year. It has been quite otherwise. And in this respect Judaism has manifested a genius of its own in sanctifying its method of reckoning time by keeping the subject entirely free from merely local or national associations. There is a loftiness in this matter and an intrinsic spirituality which of itself places the Jewish religion on the pedestal of universalism. It is not so much the anniversary of a particular day on which God performed a mighty deed, with which our devotions are awakened on the Day of Memorial, as the broad religious proposition that the God whom we worship is He who created all things.

No religion and no people are so misapprehended, even by persons who in other respects are well-informed, than Judaism and the Jewish people. Indeed the constant repetition of misstatements about Judaism have even led (it is to be feared) many born Israelites to misconceive their great inheritance and therefore to desert it. The root of these misapprehensions may be traced to the primary question as to what kind of God it is whom Israel worships. We are sometimes told it is a "tribal God," and some people foolishly imagine that He is not quite the same Being to whom other people render homage. The liturgy for the Day of Memorial abounds with descriptions of the Supreme Being which could not fail to arouse in a non-Jewish mind the consciousness that that Being is indeed the Common Father. It is worth while here to quote the language repeated in a form of confession used on that day, as also on the Day of Atonement: "Most merciful and gracious God, we have sinned against Thee, O have compassion upon us." And then those attributes which appeal to every human being are enumerated thus: " Lord of pardon, who surveyest the future, who ridest upon the heavens, who callest generations into being, who art the perfection of knowledge and who art attentive to prayer, we have sinned against Thee, O have compassion upon us." Nothing can be more catholic than this conception of our Divine Creator, and there is nothing more distinctly Jewish than that particular supplication. It is well that Jews and Jewesses should at this season see clearly that the religious system which claims their allegiance is one which is singularly illumined by its thorough comprehension of this great truth, namely, that the Creator, and the Father of the Spirits of all Flesh is the only proper object of Divine worship. That is a truth the full significance of which has yet to be appreciated by vast multitudes of people who claim to be in advance of Israel in the spiritual march. It is a truth which is tampered with, and although appearing to be so elementary among the lessons of childhood, it is just that one truth of all others which civilised nations have been most tardy in acquiring. Classic Greece and gifted Rome came and went without any large proportion of their sons ever having recognised it. Christendom with all its advance has not yet assimilated as completely as that prayer expresses that simple Hebrew conception. It is by no means certain that the idea represented in Mohammedanism and in regions of Northern and Southern Asia is quite so catholic, broad and simple as this Jewish idea of God. In China undoubtedly it is not.

What appears to me to be the one main fact to submit to my co-religionists on these great occasions is that fact which seems to stare us in the face whenever we contemplate such solemn convocations as the Day of Memorial. It is briefly this—and would that it could be audible in every Jewish soul!—Israelite! you are in fellowship with a Divine Commission; you are an Israelite in order to spread the knowledge of a true and reasonable worship of the only One perfect Being whom it is possible to conceive. Your Jewish distinctness is a means to an end. It is only a badge of your mission. Jews must be spiritual persons or their very name is meaningless. The Day of Memorial and the Day of Atonement afford special opportunities for the Jew to recuperate himself spiritually, and to become more fit for his exalted Mission. We are the hereditary guardians of a truth that is more precious than life itself. There is no single group of people who are so mysteriously and so divinely charged as the Jews throughout the world. The spread of monotheism, as Jews understand it, among civilized nations, appears to be the goal after which independent schools of philosophy are now striving. The ultimate success of their efforts largely depends upon the steadfastness of the Jewish people. Jews cannot too forcibly remind one another that they stand out in history as the one consecrated band pledged to this truth.

Is Monotheism really making way in our own time? Will the general wreck of mediæval theology leave the most cultured nations of Europe in a state of religious anarchy, or will it rather prepare them to take hold of that one Divine truth for which our race has lived and suffered through so many centuries? It is important that Jewish communities should recognise how intimately their religious position is bound up with this problem. If the Jewish religion were dissolved to-morrow and the Hebrew race were merged into other communities, there can be no doubt that the cause of monotheism among civilised men would receive a tremendous blow, and civilisation in its highest sense would be immeasurably retarded.

The Day of Memorial may be spoken of as the Great Feast of Monotheism and of Natural Religion. The story of Abraham's faith, and the recital of those parts of Scripture which specially emphasize Israel's teaching about God and His relation to the world, ought to impress every one of us with two great thoughts: What God is to us, and what we ought to be to mankind. Judaism is a missionary religion or it is nothing. It is a message to mankind, not a hidden treasure for a single people. On this point the wildest errors prevail, even among our own people. Proselytism, as popularly understood and commonly illustrated in other religious organisations, is not necessarily the way for Israel to uplift their torch; but we are none the less missionaries. Our religion must spread as soon as the conditions for spreading it are assured. The liberty of the soul, of which social and political liberty are the forerunners, is a purpose which Judaism is able to guarantee and which the Jewish people, sooner or later, are bound to teach in a direct way. A thousand years in the Divine sight are but as yesterday when it is passed. The future of Judaism is as assured as were all the political and intellectual consequences of the first Reform Act in England. This is not difficult to discern. The active propaganda by Israelites of the sacred truths they have laid up in store for thousands of years is something to be expected in the natural course of events, just as the actions of a newly enfranchised Democracy must gradually follow their enfranchisement. When the educated portion of European citizens are emancipated from the terrorism of a creed which rests upon miracle, they will be the first to seek for knowledge upon spiritual matters from the one and only historically spiritual people. This may appear a digression, but it is just one of those reflections which the recurrence of a Jewish New Year and Day of Calling to Remembrance naturally forces upon English Jews living in this advanced age. Judaism is destined to be the religion of mankind.

DENOMINATIONAL SCHOOLS *VERSUS* BOARD SCHOOLS.

[Reprinted from the "Jewish Chronicle," May 6th, 1887.]

THE Education Act of 1870, introduced by the late Mr. Forster, seems to have produced impressions upon some minds which were never contemplated by the lamented statesman, nor intended by the Act of Parliament. The institution of Board Schools was designed to meet certain requirements which were not met by the educational fabric that existed before the year 1870. Up to that time there were throughout the country most efficient schools for the children of some sections of the working classes, owing to the activity of the principal religious bodies. The Church of England (National) Schools were admirably managed, they provided for the training of a vast section of the general community. On the other hand, the Roman Catholic Church, and the various Nonconformist bodies had their schools, which were splendidly conducted, and contributed individually and collectively to the good of the community. Among the numerous denominations, the schools which the Jews provided for their own poor were in every respect among the best in the country. The sound moral training was a striking characteristic of these schools, and the secular teaching was not second in excellence to that of any school in the kingdom. There was no feature in the Jewish communal life more creditable than the excellence of their educational system. This is not difficult to account for, because history shows that education has always been one of the first efforts of the Synagogue, and it is known to be a cardinal point of the Jewish religion. Without troubling my readers with statistics that might easily be supplied, it is enough to remind them that the Church of England, the Roman Catholic Church, the Synagogue, and the various Nonconformist bodies did not numerically embrace more than some large sections of the working classes and the poor. The Catholics, the Jews, and the Methodists, certainly included in their respective folds some of the poorest strata of society. It was indeed a striking fact that the poorest and the humblest of these particular denominations were always actively conforming members of their communions. Such however, was never the case in the Church of England. Moreover there were sects, such as the Quakers and the Unitarians, who never numbered among their worshippers any considerable section of the working classes. They are both denominations of somewhat recent growth, and were the result of movements among the intellectual classes. Moreover, it has to be remembered that when we have added together all the different religious bodies we get a numerical total which falls far short of any figure that would represent the entire population of Great Britain. Indeed, there are a very large number of our fellow-subjects who have never belonged to any communion, and were therefore not within the groups of those for whom these different schools were established. It thus came about that while communities of different creeds were providing an excellent schooling for their poor, there yet remained a considerable portion of the working classes and the poor throughout the country who were not supplied with the means of education.

Those enormous numbers of untaught citizens were further increased by the fact that even among some of the religious bodies themselves it was often found that their resources were inadequate, and that in country districts and towns it was not always easy to raise enough funds to build a school in connection with a place of worship, or that the school was perhaps not large enough for the needs of the locality. This last difficulty can scarcely be said to have existed among all sects. It is tolerably certain that the Catholics and the Jews made every sacrifice to provide the number of schools that were necessary in proportion to their congregations. Whoever remembers the state of public opinion before 1870 on the subject of national education, will be able to recall the fears that were entertained, lest the proposed Board Schools should interfere with or supersede the existing denominational schools. After all, in a Constitutional Government like ours, the State is the servant, not the master. Politicians and thoughtful men have occasion to deprecate a tendency among some people to make the State the guide and censor over all public affairs. The soundest principle in politics is that the State should be the instrument in the hand of the people, and not the people in the hands of the State. The great contention in favour of the Education Bill (1870) was that it was the duty of the State to protect society from the evil consequences of having a totally illiterate mass permeating the life of the country. In the light of subsequent events, it was obviously the bounden duty of the State to see that those on whom political power was to be conferred should be able to read and write and cipher, and to acquire some degree of mental training. Some politicians regret (not without reason) that the provision did not precede that extension of political rights by at least a generation. The State was justified in levying rates for the purpose of its Board Schools in the interest of society, just as it is warranted in thus providing for police and other protection. The attitude of the Liberal Party, whose forces at that time carried Mr. Forster's Bill, was certainly that the measure was required as a matter of police regulation.

Now I venture to contrast the origin of the

Board Schools, to which "A True Conservative" was so loud in his homage, with the origin of the Jewish denominational schools which he is so eager to sacrifice. Our schools, to put it in simple language, are the outcome of our religion. They are as strongly and as distinctively the expression of our divine Law as the institution of the Sabbath or any other detail revealed in the Decalogue. It is as incumbent upon the Synagogue to provide for the education of the poor as it is to find a resting place for the Ark of the Covenant. I may be told that I am using strong language. The answer is that it becomes necessary to assert and re-assert truths which are apt to become enveloped by the superficial views of economists and the apostles of that poor charter "expediency." The instances in our history which illustrate the need for "strong language," crowd around the memory of those who are deeply conscious that Judaism would long since have perished if "expediency" had been permitted to usurp the claims of devotion.

The lax views which have been gaining ground in the last few years as to our denominational schools must be regarded as a symptom of slackening attachment to the Covenant of our fathers. This weakening of sacred convictions was manifested in a pronounced way for the first time in our community by the closing of one of our oldest schools a few years ago. It was very instructive to observe how the loss of the chief guiding spirit of the Sephardic Congregation was quickly followed by the abolition of their school. The arguments used by the "True Conservative" gained ground on that occasion, and found practical expression, ever to be lamented. But in that particular case the Board School which received the outcast pupils was to all intents and purposes a Jewish school. No head master of any Jewish school is more efficient as a teacher, nor more fervent as an Israelite than Mr. Levy of the Old Castle Street School. For this reason, and for this alone, the sixty or seventy boys were in a large measure compensated for the dissolution of their school. But such would not be the case in other instances. If, for example, the few hundreds of pupils at the Hanway Place School were dispersed among the Board Schools of London, it is tolerably certain that their dispersion would be attended by no such alleviating circumstances. On the contrary, it is evident even from the "True Conservative's" own admission that those children would be driven broadcast upon the chances and accidents inevitable at Board Schools. Even their religious instruction would depend upon the whim of individuals, and upon the haphazard teaching which an inadequately supported Association could offer. The fact that there are in the community men of substance able to subscribe £5 a year to one institution, but unwilling to support our own schools, is of itself a source of anxiety that ought to be considered. I observed that there was nothing in the letter for the case against denominational schools. The points raised were quite superficial, though, no doubt, calculated to mislead. For instance, it was contended that it would be a positive advantage for our poor children to go to Board Schools on the ground that the intercourse with children of other creeds would enlarge their views. No consideration, however, was given to the facts, which are stated at the outset of this article, that the children, for the most part, who attend Board Schools have no creed at all.

All Board School children leave the schools to earn their bread at what is, after all, but a tender age. Mostly at twelve years they have done with their schooling. Now, any enlargement of ideas and knowledge of the world that can be imparted from one set of children to another under the age of twelve, especially of the kind of children who attend Board Schools, may be described as a species of knowledge which it would be to the distinct advantage of the children to be without, and from which it is our duty to protect them. Unhappily, the poor little things go into the world rather too soon as it is, and, for my own part, I would gladly see them sheltered from that knowledge of the world which the "True Conservative" thinks so desirable. His illustration of the argument was somewhat grotesque when he compared the case of these children with those who are sent to public schools and Universities. In the first place, boys are not admitted at Eton, Harrow, Rugby, and the other public schools, till they have passed twelve years, prior to which they have been carefully and studiously guarded from the very kind of intercourse referred to. Meanwhile, in cultivated homes they acquire with much greater facility all the religious instruction which our denominational schools provide for our poor, where homes cannot supply it. In some of the instances to which the "True Conservative" alludes, the "children" did not go to school at all. They were educated by private tuition, and there was invariably one experienced Jewish teacher to teach them Hebrew. As to the Universities, the "children" cannot enter before they are seventeen or eighteen, and the sort of "knowledge" which they get is not of the "world" in the sense of which the correspondent speaks, but a knowledge quite of one side of the world—the intellectual, the literary, and the sporting world. It is only necessary to disprove one of the analogies which a "True Conservative" seeks to draw in order to awaken a distrust as to the soundness in his process of reasoning.

The letter of a "True Conservative" repeats the threadbare, empty fallacy about *first an Englishman, then a Jew.* It is surprising how much nonsense can be spoken on this subject. The real facts are these: Whoever believes in religion must inevitably hold that the claims of religion are paramount. Neither the national nor any other sentiment can exert an influence so remarkable. In fact, from the very nature of the religious idea, it must supersede every other. A Christian is first a Christian and then an Englishman. Even a churchman or a Catholic or a Wesleyan gives his first allegiance to his religious communion. As to Judaism, the whole character of our religion places God and the service of God before and above all other objects. Perhaps it is more exact to say that in the Jewish religion God and the service of God include or embrace all other objects. Hence, it is absurd to single out one of the objects of life, however important, and say this is greater than the one which includes it and gives it what is best about it. Those Jews who proceed with making their children first Englishmen or Frenchmen, as the case may be, and afterwards Jews, have failed to grasp the intention of religion generally, and the office of Judaism in particular. Of all religions there is none which so completely controls all the impulses and affections of human life as the religion of the Bible. That is its genius—its far reaching and transcendent prerogative. Again, patriotism, political morality, love of one's country, and good citizenship, are virtues which, to every man, except an Atheist, derive their culture from the religious idea which underlies them. Some religions are better suited to the development of these virtues than others. But it has been the contention of our race, in all ages, that the Jewish religion is singularly fertile with the growth of these very virtues, so we are justified in stating that to make a child a good Israelite is to insure his becoming a good citizen.

This talk about "an Englishman first and a Jew afterwards" is just as shallow as such a doctrine as this: First make a man a faithful husband, and then make him a good man afterwards. The whole value of any religion depends upon its power of promoting in man all the virtues that are necessary to a well-ordered life. Those to whom the chief pride of life consists in their nationality are of two kinds, either those on whom religion has very little hold, or religious people who do not reflect in a logical manner, but are accustomed to think in a slipshod fashion. It will be an evil day for Israel, and consequently for the interests of human progress, when this notion of setting the two sentiments of religion and patriotism in rivalry becomes general. It is quite easy, of course, to comprehend the attitude of those who know little and believe less in the sacred mission to which our race is permanently dedicated; but it is quite impossible to account for this contention in the minds of Israelites who know their history and believe in their mission. As a matter of fact there is no more sense in placing in competition the two sentiments of patriotism and religious allegiance than there is in comparing any other two interests which have no reason to clash one with the other. A true patriotic Englishman is as capable of devotion to the Synagogue as he is to the Church; and yet he is justified in regarding the privilege of being born an Israelite with a different set of emotions from those which surround his ideas of patriotism. It is an historical fact, by far the most precious that our ancestors have bequeathed to us, that whenever the extraordinary choice was thrust upon them between patriotism and religious allegiance, the best of them selected the latter whilst the ignoble ones chose the former. We are much more proud of those Spanish Jews who preferred Judaism to Spain than the other Spanish Jews who sacrificed their religion for their country. So in this very century, in Great Britain, there is no comparison between the characters of the men who got baptised in order to gain citizenship and the disposition of the others who continued aliens in order to preserve their religion. These encounters, of course, were never of our own choosing, nor need they be calculated upon in the ordinary reckoning of human probabilities, but they have occurred, and they may recur in other countries. The true test of this question is the conduct of men under such extreme conditions. And, judged by the light of past events and future contingencies, it is obvious that Jews who say that they are first Englishmen and then Jews are either false to their mission or else they are talking nonsense.

The preservation of our religion is the supreme duty of all Jews who believe in Judaism. The first act incumbent on us is to teach the Mosaic Law to our children. Hence it is not merely that we have to provide education for the poor of our race, but we have to provide a particular kind of education. For this purpose it is indispensable that we should have our own schools, conducted in our own way, and not according to any Act of an English, French, or German Parliament. The moment we give up these schools, and suffer our poor to attend the Parliamentary institutions of the day, we become guilty of the greatest act of neglect and wilful disobedience to our divine Law of which, in the circumstances of the present day, we are capable. It would not be worth while to remain a Jew for one week if there was not in Judaism a vitality and a purpose worthy of sacrifice. There is no more ignoble tendency in a people who have fought and won religious liberty than voluntarily to surrender that for which their fathers have struggled. I venture to suggest that it would be quite reasonable that every member of a congregation should be assessed in order to provide the means for maintaining as many Jewish schools as are necessary to include the entire number of our poor. But in the absence of such assessment it is right to expect that every Jew and Jewess who has the means will not shrink from the most sacred obligation to maintain the Jewish education of their poor.

It will be apparent that the foregoing observations were called forth by a controversy in regard to the maintenance of a particular denominational school. The reason why I have thought it fitting to reprint the article in this volume, is that the subject is one of growing importance to the present and the rising generations. Since the year 1887, when this article appeared in the *Jewish Chronicle*, the whole question of Board Schools *versus* Denominational Schools has become more prominent. The abolition of school fees, by which the principle of free education has been established, has naturally increased the burdens of the ratepayer. The existence of Denominational voluntary schools is in some measure threatened, owing to compulsory competition with Board Schools.

MAN'S RELATION TO GOD.

A Sermon preached on שבת בראשית (*Saturday, October 3rd, 1885), at the South Hackney Synagogue.*

וַיִּבְרָא אֱלֹהִים אֶת־הָאָדָם בְּצַלְמוֹ :
"So God created man in His own image."—*Genesis* i. 27.

IF we were asked to quote one sentence from the Bible which presents an essential basis of our religion, and sets forth in a single phrase the genius of our inherited Faith, we should cite this remarkable statement from the first section of our Law, which gives the name to the present Sabbath. All that follows in our sacred literature is a superstructure upon this basis of the relation between man and his Creator. Quite true, my brethren, that the unity of God is the keynote of Judaism; but, if it were not for our affinity with the Supreme Being, His oneness would not have that attraction and significance which are so striking to the Israelite. It is said of the Jewish religion that it makes very little demand upon the faculty of belief; that whereas other religious systems are distinguished by their creeds and theology, ours is one of statutes and laws, and requires us to believe nothing except that God is one. This proposition lets in a flood of ideas, involving a philosophical inquiry with which I do not mean to trouble you. The question of belief, as distinct from faith, is a matter which has interested many thoughtful men. The comparison and the analysis of the two ideas would form a larger subject for consideration than is possible or desirable within the limits of a sermon. This much, however, we should bear in mind, when we are considering our relation to God: Faith, by which we perceive it, is so far different from belief, that it is to the Israelite an inborn capacity for recognising his spiritual tie with God, and does not, like belief, depend upon the proof which is needed in the case of one of those abstract and historic statements which is not within the easy apprehension of the soul. To a Jew, the idea of the fatherhood of God is as natural as a mother's love is to a child. A child has not to pass through any process of reasoning to become convinced of its mother's love—it feels, it knows. So to us, the idea of man's being created in the image of God comes without effort either of argument or imagination. In addressing a Jewish congregation, therefore, upon the relation of man to God, I am justified in taking for granted that you agree with me that God is really our Father, and that we are bound to Him by spiritual ties. That being so, you may ask—what, then, is there to be said? My answer is—we may take counsel together as to the mode of thinking and the manner of conduct which that faith implies and claims. We will trace the course of life which we should desire to live if the consciousness of our tie with God is to produce upon our lives, and through us upon society generally, the results which ought to follow. Let us take some instances of lives so ordered that they afford illustrations of likeness to God. There are lives in history, and within our personal experiences which seem to be inspired and guided by a motive so high and so great that we are able to discern in them the Divine Image. What we may term "the Spirit of God" is visible in some characters in a manner so striking that their example demonstrates the way to live in accordance with the high origin of our humanity. Those who have a knowledge of the poor in this vast metropolis, and of agricultural labourers, will have come in contact with lives so darkened by the conditions in which they subsist, so excluded from the ordinary means of worldly pleasure, that a wonder is aroused at the brightness and contentment which seem sometimes to lighten their gloomy pilgrimage. What is the reason of this brightness and contentment? There is certainly nothing in the external circumstances to produce a happy countenance—severe toil, physical strain, long hours, and, in London, depressing atmosphere, scant wages, homes without comfort—deficient even in necessaries;—all this accompanied with domestic responsibilities, and not always with domestic solace! Yet the victims of such a lot toil on and persevere with brave hearts, though the future may be darker than the present, for in the case of thousands of well-spent lives, there is little prospect of rest, and no better destination in this world than the work-house. In drawing this picture of life as it is, it must be observed that the burdens of the poor are not to be defended; for, indeed, they are, to a large extent, the failure of a social and political system which is amenable to treatment. But the courage with which the burden is borne—the heroism that deals with it and masters it—these indicate the dignity of human nature pointing to our divine kinship. Those lives have within them a vision which sees beyond and above the awful surroundings; they appear to know that they belong to God and not to the world—that their battle is temporary but their peace is everlasting. To come nearer home, regard the case of one of the poorest of our own brothers—an exile from Russia or Poland, coming from a persecuting land to one which he has heard is free. He brings no substance, he is ignorant of the language, "as a man dumb with silence." He finds that he adds one more to an already overstocked labour market. Just consider his moral condition, and what has brought him to this pitiful state! First, in his native land, true to his race, he resigned opportunities, and surrendered possibilities for his God. That man had only to play a part and all would have been well with him in this world. But no! with the strong heart of a martyr he resisted the foe, and adhered to his standard regardless of consequences, and in the face of dangers which are enough to terrify the brave. When he arrives in the free country a new warfare begins, he has to find bread for his family, and only God knows his difficulty. Restricted by conscience, many fields of industry are fenced to him; combined circumstances reduce to a minimum the resources of labour. And yet, after a comparatively short time, this man and a handful of others like him will form themselves into a "holy congregation," what we call in the East-end of London a "Chevrah." Their chief aim throughout is to be true to their hereditary charge according to the light that is in them. I am only stating the case when I attribute all that courage, all that devotion, the unselfishness and purity of motive to the fact that the Image of God is a conscious reality. In the life of our down-trodden, exiled brother we perceive an example of some of those great qualities which go to build up a powerful state. There is self-denial, public spirit, loyalty, courage and endurance. All these things in his case do most certainly proceed from his relation to God. He is in covenant with his Creator; he believes that he is charged by Him with a great mission to his fellow-men, and with that faith he endures—though, perhaps, he has never articulated to himself his motives and principles.

My brothers and sisters! this place reminds me that there is close at hand an illustration of the action upon human conduct of the Image of God. Here is a society of faithful men who have worked and sacrificed for a holy cause. Few in number, and not enriched in the things of the world, an ambition took root among you to contribute your share of service to the ancient army of Israel, and you have done it loyally. You have provided schools for the rearing of your children in the grand Faith which you inherit, and which you rightly conceive it is your duty and your privilege to transmit. You have organised one more congregation to the honour of our community, and have provided many individuals in this populous district with a centre of "holy convocation." To accomplish such a work against all impediments required a tone of mind and a condition of heart which were not of this world. There is an inner consciousness which has aroused you, and that is the likeness of God within you.

Upon most subjects there are differences of opinion. Religion, being nearest the heart of man, has excited a wide diversion. There are some matters, however, even in the sphere of religion, in regard to which there is rather a different aspect than a difference of opinion. There can be no difference of opinion among our own people as to the Shemang Yisrael and the constitution of our Faith, but there may be a difference of views. That is to say, Jews, like other men, vary in the degree of their appreciation of their ancestral Faith, and they also vary in the estimate they make of the duties which their religion demands. To speak with perfect frankness as a man to his kinsmen, it is very questionable whether we all rise to the height of our position as God's "Kingdom of Priests," His "Witnesses," and whether many of us do not substitute for our exalted Faith the mere observance of forms and ceremonies. Are we not disposed to judge the proficiency of a Jewish life by the extent to which outward observances are seen? Does a good Jew mean a man who rigidly adheres to all the ceremonial of Judaism, or one who carries through life as an active principle the consciousness that God created him in His own Image? I do not for a moment mean to imply that the Jew who is rigidly observant need on that account be less spiritual, for it is quite certain that some of the most observant rabbins have literally lived with God on earth; but what ought to be made clear is that the evidence of true Judaism does not rest with outward observances. It is possible to be scrupulous in regard to all the ordinances of the Synagogue, and yet to have failed utterly in the spiritual grasp of the Jewish religion—never to have risen to the sublimity of our hereditary Faith, and at the same time, from habit or association, or even from superstition, to have fulfilled every detail in the ritual observances. We cannot be too cautious to keep the standard of a Jewish life as high as possible, and to be vigilant in our fear of the danger of suffering that standard to fall from the height at which Almighty God placed it. In the sentence before us we find that the greatest spiritual truth known to mankind was laid down as the basis of Judaism—namely, affinity with the Supreme Being! Consequently a moral idea for human conduct in harmony with the Divine nature. This constitutes the standard of a Jewish life, and nothing short of it is the goal for each Israelite, if he will fulfil his mission and be true to his calling. We are all "priests" in the sight of God, and in the expectation of the world. No wonder if God is wroth, and the world is surprised, when we fall short. Human weaknesses are to be taken into account for Jews as well as for other men; but a just fear lies also in another cause. Our history, unlike the history of other religions, is not laden with creeds, and therefore we are not threatened with the danger of too much belief; but we are subjected to another kind of error: circumstances have added to the Jewish religion a great many observances, and the standard of Judaism is sometimes missed by mistaking those observances for the religion itself. In making these remarks, I am not advocating any specific change in our ritual. Change has been too often mistaken for progress; and to relax observance does not necessarily mean spiritual advance,—indeed it has nothing to do with it. It is the attitude of mind towards these things that should be considered. Give things their true proportion, and their proper place, and they will fulfil their purpose. It cannot be too emphatically declared from the Jewish pulpit that the first requirements of Judaism are those which shall conform with the faith that lies at the root of it all, namely, that "God created man in His own Image," and man is required, therefore, to live after the likeness of God,—in other words, his object in life must be to develop a moral character by cultivating qualities which are God-like. You are familiar with the expression a "God-like" man, or a "God-like" woman. It is said of some of the heroes of our race "he walked with God." We might all of us cast our lives in a God-like manner. The whole burden of moral teaching in our Scriptures is this exhortation to Godliness. Throughout the Levitical Law, Almighty God is represented as the Crown, as it were, of the Moral Empire: "Be ye holy: for I the Lord your God am holy" (Leviticus xix. 2); and "Fear thy God: I am the Lord" (Leviticus xix. 14, 32). "For I, the Lord your God which sanctify you, am holy" (Leviticus xxi. 8). Against many moral injunctions respecting our duties in this world, we have the divine motive before us in the words, אני יהוה אלהיכם, "I am the Lord your God." This constant reference to God is the very "Holy of Holies" in the Jewish religion קדוש הקדשים. Our prophets, from the great Isaiah down to Malachi, agree in making God the motive for human conduct, thus showing our affinity with Him and His nearness to us. "Can a woman forget her sucking child? Yea, they may forget, yet will I not forget thee" (Isaiah xliv. 5). Then we have that typical prayer which connects the mind of man with the Spirit of God: "Thou will keep him in perfect peace whose mind is stayed on Thee, because he trusteth in Thee" (Isaiah xxvi. 3). Again, the Prophet Malachi saw the precious tie which binds human souls to their Maker: "Then they that feared the Lord spake often one to another and the Lord hearkened and heard it, and a book of remembrance was written before Him for them that feared the Lord, and that *thought* upon His name; and they shall be mine, saith the Lord, in that day when I make up my jewels; and I will spare him as a man spareth his own son" (Malachi iii. 16). So in our daily life may we not put the question to ourselves concerning our actions and our motives: *Is this like God? Is that God-like?* Such a course of spiritual training, if widely extended, would remove from society those evils with which it is afflicted. Deceit, selfishness, avarice, and all uncharitableness would become annihilated. On the other hand, honesty of purpose, human sympathy, and a keen sense of justice would prevail. Purity of heart and freedom from corruption would be the characteristics of any society or of any single life which sought always God as the motive and the inspiration. We must all be preachers and ministers of God one to another; and here, I should like to say how much there is to be accomplished in our own community to keep the public conscience rightly sensitive. There must not be found in Israel a dishonest man nor a bad woman! This can be prevented, I feel sure, by a steadfast care for the young and for the poor of our race.

There is one more view of this subject, my brethren, that I cannot withhold from you, and which I would ask you to consider. If all men are created in the Image of God, then it must occur to you that there is an extraordinary bond between man and man. In my judgment, that bond is so strong that it far outweighs any other considerations which cause social and human differences, such as those arising from distinct nationalities, separate races, and different creeds or parties. Human brotherhood is part of that very essential basis of religion, for it springs from the fatherhood of God. It is difficult to understand the state of mind which bends in homage before the Almighty Father, and yet stands up in hostility towards a fellow-creature, because some chance partition happens to be between them. Class distinction, marked by artificial lines, such as those which make a difference between the rich and the poor are utterly wrong in the light of this teaching. Social and personal prejudices amount to a denial of human brotherhood, and we shall not properly appreciate our relations to God, till we all live in more perfect union with one another. The rich have much to learn from the poor, and the poor have a right to expect a great deal from the rich. Some men see a realisation of human brotherhood in all kinds of political schemes; but of one thing we may be certain,—if we cling to the faith that we all are created in the image of God, and that true godliness of life is the goal for every man, there need be no fear as to the future of society and the human race.

The moral enthusiasm of the Israelite cannot be quenched, when he has for his inspiration the powerful reflection that "God created man in His own Image." The Hebrew Liturgy lifts our thoughts to a contemplation of the Divine attributes, so that at our devotions we may call to mind those characteristics of the Divine nature which it is possible for us to imitate. In the morning service you remember the ברוך שאמר, "Blessed be He who sayeth and performeth. Blessed be He who hath compassion upon all creatures. Blessed be He in whom there is neither respect of persons nor taking of bribes. He is righteous in all His ways, and merciful in all His works." This is said of God, but it may surely be said of men too! A human being who is made after the likeness of God, whether he be Jew or Gentile, may pursue an earthly career which these words would describe; he too can be faithful; he also may have compassion "upon all creatures," without "respect of persons," or "taking of bribes"; and he may be "righteous in all his ways," and "benevolent in all his works." Within the last forty-eight hours, a life such as this has passed to eternal rest. Such was the character of our illustrious fellow-countryman—one of the greatest figures of this century. Lord Shaftesbury was distinguished by those very points which indicate that "God created man in His own Image." How widely soever we may differ from any opinion of his, this is the true description of his life, from which no right-thinking person can dissent. Our own venerable champion, too, Sir Moses Montefiore, who passed away with the fall of summer, was indeed such a man who lived with God, and cultivated, in a high degree, those attributes which in the Deity are worshipped.

Whoever wishes to know how, in practical life, he can live after the likeness of God, he will find the exact description of such a life in one of our Kippur Psalms (xv.)—"He that walketh uprightly, and worketh righteousness, and speaketh the truth in his heart: he that backbiteth not with his tongue, nor doeth evil to his neighbour; in whose eye a vile person is contemned, but he honoureth them that fear the Lord; he that sweareth to his own hurt, and changeth not; he that putteth not out his money to usury, nor taketh a bribe against the innocent; he that doeth these things shall never be moved." In other words, he is God-like.

O my brethren! it is for us to make this perfect Judaism the universal religion of mankind, by setting forth in our lives the example of such Godliness. If we ourselves so live, we can make others live likewise. How different would be the tone of society if this were the universal code. A purity would obtain in public life; politics would not be divorced from religion; every man who seeks a public career would have the image of God before him to guide his conduct. In private life there would be a constant probing of actions and motives. We act from various motives, but are they always the highest? Transparency in every dealing and business transaction is required by the Jewish religion. We see, then, that the words "God created man in his own Image" are the real source of moral action, the true guide to personal holiness, the vital basis of religion.

THE MISSION OF ISRAEL.

Sermon delivered at the Spanish and Portuguese Synagogue in Manchester, on Saturday, 1st January, 1887.

וְיָדְעוּ הַגּוֹיִם כִּי אֲנִי יְהֹוָה מְקַדֵּשׁ אֶת־יִשְׂרָאֵל בִּהְיוֹת מִקְדָּשִׁי בְּתוֹכָם לְעוֹלָם:

"And the nations shall know that I the Lord do sanctify Israel, when my sanctuary shall be in the midst of them for evermore."—*Ezekiel* xxxvii. 28.

WHEN an Israelite attains his religious majority at the age fixed by ancient Hebrew usage, he is received into the full fellowship of Israel as a responsible member of the congregation. The sacred army of Israel is thus recruited from generation to generation by the sons and heirs of the holy Covenant. The divine inheritance and the noble traditions of the race are handed down from father to son, thereby securing permanence in the world of that "Kingdom of Priests and Holy Nation" which was called and sanctified in early days of human history. Those of the house of Israel who have already reached the age of maturity, and who have had the time and the opportunity to understand the full significance of their racial position in the world, must be stirred with anxious hopes as to those who are to come after them. Those of us who have estimated the influence of our race upon mankind, and who have formed solemn convictions as to the will of God concerning us, must look into the future with a longing desire that the generations to come may be worthy of our illustrious ancestry, who took the lead in the structure of that universal edifice which is called civilisation. We must indeed be eager to see some assurance in our own time that the links in the chain of our sacred history may pass on one by one, not only unimpaired, but replenished in strength and brightness, so that the refining furnace through which so many of them have emerged may tell their tale on the future of our people.

There are many events in life which, from their frequent recurrence, are apt to lose their influence. In the course of the year a Jewish congregation is accustomed to see so many of their younger brethren go through the ceremony of Bar Mitzva, or Confirmation, that they, as well as the youths, are likely to regard such incidents as mere formalities. If it could be conceived that the whole destiny of our race depended upon the Bar Mitzva of each single youth, the ceremonial would naturally excite the same interest and enthusiasm which have been manifested at times when the life of the Synagogue seemed to be threatened. But I submit that although an isolated event like that which we have witnessed to-day is not of itself associated with apprehensions of that kind, it is one of those circumstances which, in combination, does seriously relate both to the past and to the future of Judaism. Whilst the individual case of Bar Mitzva is full of significance and tender association to more than one person, the act as an institution is of vital issue to all Israel. It is the symbol of the commission which God has placed in the hands of every Israelite. It is the recognition and the assumption of the duties, which by reason of our birth, all Israelites are summoned to perform in obedience to that early command in Exodus, " ye shall be unto me a kingdom of priests and a holy nation."

A child who is born a king does not, before a certain age, assume the functions of the crown. When the time comes that he is to take upon himself the kingly office, the occasion is full of importance to his dynasty, and to the state over which he is to reign. Meanwhile, he is carefully protected and trained to discharge the obligations of his high calling. In a kingdom of another kind, and of a holy character, each Israelite is born a priest of the kingdom of priests, with definite functions to discharge, not only in relation to his own communion, but, in a wider sense, to mankind. In his childhood he has been guarded, and sheltered, and instructed by the unsurpassed love of a Jewish mother. Everything has been done to guarantee his fitness for the duties that await him. The Mosaic code, as well as the love of devoted parents, provide that care, physical as well as moral, which are to effect such salutary results on the life of a Jew. Fully equipped with the education required at his age, and able to read the Law, he is presented to the congregation, and for the first time takes his part in the public service. He becomes a soldier of the covenant of Israel. On such an occasion he is bidden to go and be one of the "kingdom of priests," one of the "holy nation." We, who tell him this, are reminded of the sanctity of Israel, and the effect of that sanctity upon the world. This is why I have chosen these remarkable words of the prophet, which declare that the nations shall know that it was the Eternal who sanctified us, and that that knowledge should be complete when His sanctuary is seen to be in the midst of us for evermore. According to the prophetic utterance the condition of our work in the world is clearly that we ourselves shall be sanctified. What is meant by our being sanctified? Is it not the same idea that we find again and again expressed in our Book of Books? "Thou art an holy people unto me." "Be ye holy, for I the Lord your God am holy." "I have called thee in righteousness." "Thou art a peculiar treasure unto me." "Ye are my witnesses, saith the Lord." "Ye shall be my people, and I will be your God."

My brethren! the true meaning of God's sanctuary being in the midst of Israel is this, and I ask you to follow the argument. We were chosen, as I have said, to take the lead in the civilisation of mankind. Other people have had their share, too, in the work of progress and culture. The Egyptians, the Greeks, and the Romans have each, in their turn, laid on stone after stone in that colossal work. No man would be true to history, and to the instincts of culture, if he denied the place which is due to the genius of the ancient Greeks in the hierarchy of universal teaching. What they have taught can only be justly appreciated by those whose minds have been steeped in the refinements of literature and art. Philosophy, logic, and geometry, as well as poetry and sculpture, owe their origin almost, but certainly their growth, to the masters of ancient Greece. The science of politics, the art of government and jurisprudence, come from the memorable institutions of ancient Rome. But, brethren, the work that was allotted to Israel was even of larger scope and of deeper consequences, for it was nothing less than the unfolding to man of that which was best within him. It was the awakening of the human conscience to its hitherto unknown power, its God-like capacity. Our share in the work of civilisation covered the entire range of moral responsibility and human conduct; and human conduct, remember, has been pronounced by the most competent critics of the age to be three-fourths of life. Our sphere was preeminently a holy one, for it was the teaching, and the development of the holiest elements in human nature. We, by the will of Heaven, have taught mankind the exalted truth that man was created in the Image of God. We have, moreover, been permitted to illustrate the ways by which the ladder is raised from earth to heaven. It was the heroes of our race whose fame excelled the classic luminaries of Greece and Rome. It is our literature, my brethren, which has become, throughout Europe at least, the acknowledged "*Word of God.*" The compositions of the Hebrew psalmists have become the vehicles of worship in the temples of a thousand sects. Behind all forms of religious belief in Europe, in America, and in parts of Asia, and even in Africa, the race of Israel stands as the permanent prop, and the inspiration, the everflowing spring, whence is drawn as from a mighty well in countless different streams, the waters of faith, hope, and charity, the sources of history, tradition, and authority. There is no essentially religious idea in Christendom or in Mohammedanism which does not owe its birth to the Jewish Religion. These are facts, the import of which concerns all civilised men. They have their bearing upon many nations and various creeds. But for ourselves they have the most sacred meaning. I will venture to describe, in the presence of one who has this moment accepted the obligations of the manhood of Israel, what that meaning is, what indeed, should be the aim of every one who bears the Jewish name. We men and women of Israel, the "chosen" of God, His missionaries to the world, must not rest till our name becomes synonymous with the highest virtues, the fullest example of righteousness. People not of our covenant are warranted in looking to us to find moral rectitude and high spiritual life, and they may be reasonably surprised if they fail to discover that in the life of an Israelite perfect righteousness has the first claim. When it is perceived that every Jew and Jewess, or certainly the vast majority of our number, are setting an example which all the world can follow, there will be distinct evidence that the Divine Sanctuary abides amongst us. No nation will venture to doubt that it was Almighty God who thus sanctified us from the first, because we shall bear the testimony in ourselves. What is to be understood by the inspired words is nothing short of this high ideal. It needs a great effort, no doubt, to grasp it. A young Israelite, with all the advantages of a pure upbringing, in the freshness of his youth, is quite able to rise high enough in his aspirations, I maintain, to take hold of this ideal and make it his own. It is the supreme lesson which he has to learn at this eventful juncture in his career. It is the armour of truth with which he is to set out on the mission, which, by his profession of faith, he has undertaken. Whoever ventures to speak to a younger brother on his reception into the congregation of his people is bound to tell him the truth, the whole truth, and nothing but the truth, concerning the office of his race and the duties it demands of him.

Well, brethren, if I were content to say to him: From to-day forward you are expected to observe all the customs and ceremonials of Judaism, and there end, I should be giving him quite an imperfect idea, and a very misleading one, of what it is to be an Israelite. For we can quite conceive (can we not?) that a man may rigorously observe every ordinance which our traditions supply and yet exhibit a type of character as unlike the ideal presented by the prophet, as if he were no Jew at all. Mere observance of outward forms may be practised by a person who is selfish, sensual, narrow, and sectarian. In fact, ritual observance of itself, unsupported by high spiritual motives and noble conduct, does in reality often become a fetishism, and the garb of a life utterly unworthy of a dignified noble race. The Hebrew prophets have over and over again denounced Jews of this sort, and boldly told them that their practices were "an abomination unto the Lord." It is quite within human experience to find people magnifying the efficacy of outward forms to the extent that the true morality of life and the spiritual life itself are ignored. Now, I should be the last one to deprecate the use of external rites. They are thoroughly necessary, and, with a great historic religion like ours, they are indispensable; but remember that, important as they are, they are but the outer shell of what really constitutes religion itself. As the outer courts of the temple were to the "Holy place" and the "Holy of Holies," so are these observances and rites to the higher Judaism which is binding upon us. If you read the teaching of Isaiah, Jeremiah, Ezekiel, and the other prophets, not to mention the message of the Scribes, Ezra and Nehemiah, you will find that in what they had to say of Judaism, they were all agreed, differing only in language, in treatment, and in the occasion of their speech. Their description of the Jewish religion is spiritual and moral absolutely. I use the word absolutely because there is no passage in the writings attributed to them which could authorise the assumption that the religion which they taught was any other but the purest conception of ethics and the highest spirituality which has ever been taught. If I were not born a Jew and I turned to the Hebrew prophets to inquire what Judaism was, the one impression would be that it was pre-eminently a system of spiritual life and of practical morality. Well, brethren, a spiritual life and practical morality are what I have already described to be leading features in civilisation. They are conditions without which no state is wholly civilised. One state is more civilised than another in proportion to its measure of spiritual life and practical morality. Well, these highest gifts of civilisation, destined for all mankind, have been deposited in the keeping of a small group of people, " the fewest of all peoples "; deposited not to stay there alone, but to be disseminated among all men and nations. We are that people, and it is our mission to present and to extend the light of eternal truth. To preserve intact the divine truths committed to us, and to spread them far and wide, is the mission of our race. Whoever is concerned in this dissemination of divine truths must himself be first a reasonable illustration of them. That is a proposition strictly within the lines of what is intelligent, just and reasonable. For a Jew to fail in illustrating, by his own character and conduct, the spiritual life and practical morality, is to be false to his mission. The greatest enemy of our race is the born Israelite whose life is immoral. He is a distortion of what God meant him to be; and if with his ignoble life he adheres to the outward forms of our religion he makes the matter ten-fold worse, for then he becomes a traitor in the camp.

It cannot be necessary to explain in detail what is meant by practical morality. The Mosaic law is so explicit on this matter that there is no condition of human affairs where the right road is not indicated and clearly distinguished from the wrong one. But there is a point of elevation in practical morality which enters into that other department of religion which I have called the spiritual life. Morality, as you are aware, has two aspects, the one is action, and the other is motive. Now, the motive for action varies in different systems of life. The motive for action in Judaism is this high spirituality which I have mentioned. To illustrate my meaning I would say, that to be truthful and to bear honest witness is a moral act, but the motive for such conduct may be of different value. It may be in obedience to the law of the land to avoid the penalty of perjury. It may be the law of society which is conventional, and only causes a shrinking from the odium of social unpopularity. Neither of these two motives is spiritual. But there is the third motive which is spiritual. It is of deepest root and most profound in its influence, namely—that source of action which springs from the attributes of God Himself, that is to say, to act as God would act, believing that you are created in His Image, and therefore must resemble in your mortal way His Divine nature. It is His nature to be true, hence you must be truthful. This motive is independent of all selfish or social reasons, and has reference only to your relation to God. If a man were in a state of isolation, screened from the eye, and freed from the fetters of social judgment, with this spiritual motive he will harbour nothing in his mind that would be inconsistent with his relation to God. This is the spiritual side of religion, and it is the transcendent part of it. It rests upon the faith which we inherit in the Eternal God of perfect righteousness. We can consciously cultivate the fruits of this faith by referring every action and thought to the tribunal of His infinite goodness. The great value of the worship of God, which is such a prominent feature in the Jewish religion, is this very cultivation of our kinship with God—the lifting up of the mind and heart into the presence of His everlasting light, thus recuperating that heart and mind with the knowledge and strength of Divine Wisdom. This is the very pinnacle of the faith of an Israelite. It is part of the inmost sanctuary or the " Holy of Holies " of the Jewish religion.

People who are not Jews often endeavour and succeed in acquiring that practical morality founded on this high spiritual life, but they will invariably tell you that they have derived all their knowledge of these highways from the direct teaching of the Hebrew prophets, and from the living examples of the heroes of our race ; and even where they claim for the founders of their religion some names which are not included in the list of those whom the Synagogue counts its prophets, they never seek to deny, but always strenuously insist, that the Hebrew prophets, and they alone, were the teachers of their teachers. Indeed, their great effort has ever been to establish an identity of teaching between their teachers and ours. Upon the hypothesis that the two agree, do they rely for the actual authority of their own? The finest philanthropy of the present age, the noblest instances of pure unselfish life are admittedly the offspring of some religious faith which claims its descent from the Faith of Israel. Here again you see, my brethren, the tremendous influence of our race upon the world, aye, and upon the best portion of human society. With this influence, I contend, comes its obligations, obligations binding in every age upon every Jew and Jewess. Does not this thought rebound upon us with the awful sense of what we owe to God, to ourselves, and to the world? Though the vicissitudes of our peculiar history have thrown us back in the full exercise of our work as active missionaries of God, and encased us for a time in a forced separateness which has excluded our sages from going forth unreservedly to preach religion to the Gentiles, so inscrutable was the decree of Providence in first calling us His "Kingdom of Priests," His "Witnesses," that our teaching has perceptibly gone forth from age to age, and has brought about results which the student of history cannot exaggerate, results deeply affecting the highest department in the civilisation of nations, and forcing upon peoples and upon churches words which I might be justified in quoting from their own writings, declaring that the kinsmen of our race brought Divine Light to them.

With this statement of the actual position of the Synagogue in the world, accompanied by definitions of Judaism in its highest aspect, I submit that to take upon oneself the full fellowship of Israel is to enter into the most solemn covenant of fidelity to God, loyalty to his race, and to take upon himself the spirit of a missionary towards the world. Races and communities are but the combined forces of individual life. Some people erroneously consider that, as by a kind of miracle, the conduct of a whole people is different in kind from the action of an individual; and that the character and repute of a public body has nothing to do with the personal character and repute of a single member of it. But in truth the only practical way by which we can raise the tone and heighten the reputation of an entire people is by the individual struggle to improve ourselves. The only true guide for a community gifted with the lofty ideals of our race is by each one of us setting about the work of life as if upon him alone depended the fame and honour of Israel. Thus there is a value in this old custom of ours of taking our younger brethren singly through this act of Bar Mitzva or Confirmation. It individualises the teaching we have to convey. It emphasises the individuality of Jewish obligations.

Upon you, my young brother, rests, as upon the whole House of Israel, the personal obligation to do your utmost to maintain the justice of the Jewish cause by pursuing a course of life in strict obedience to our Divine commands. Into your keeping is confided from to-day the fair name of the Synagogue. Remember that God has declared, and has never annulled the declaration, that we are His "Witnesses." We knew Him before any other people had a knowledge of Divine Revelation. You belong to the oldest of God's standard-bearers and are one of them. Your future life, which we pray may be long spared in health and vigour, will be a distinct factor in the life of Israel. Let us, my brethren, all unite in one combined effort to discharge worthily the glorious mission of our race—to keep intact our wonderful inheritance and our great traditions, and set forth by the highest example the " beauty of holiness." Then shall we have for ever His sanctuary in the midst of us, and all the nations shall know that it was the eternal God who sanctified Israel for the good of mankind.

THE DIVINE PRESENCE.

[Sermon delivered at West Hampstead, April 26th, 1890.]

"And he said, My presence shall go with thee, and I will give thee rest."—*Exodus* xxxiii. 14.

"Cast me not away from thy presence; and take not thy holy spirit from me."—*Psalm* li. 11.

THESE two passages, taken from different parts of the Bible, and presenting the devout aspiration of two of the foremost figures in religious history, seem to open before us the inmost sanctuary of the Jewish religion. The assurance to Moses and the prayer of David—two men singularly unlike one another, who probably had nothing in common except their religious faith, convey to us a sense of something like concurrent testimony to the deepest truths, and testimony of the highest possible value. For who can speak about the Presence of God, and those deeper thoughts belonging to the realm of faith with greater authority than the founder of Judaism, on the one hand, and the illustrious Hebrew poet king on the other? Their views about God and about the human relationship with the Divine Being must necessarily carry a weight which would not attach to any other figure in Hebrew history if we except the prophet Isaiah. Whereas there has been some divergence between the views of the founders of other religions, and those of their immediate followers upon what is generally called theology, it is a matter of much significance that there is an absolute unity of thought between Moses and his followers who were separated from him by an enormous gulf of time and circumstance. Although the book of Psalms contains far more numerous utterances of prayer and fervid spiritual aspiration than is found in any other part of the Bible, and though some of us may be disposed to see a development of the religious idea from one stage of Jewish history to another, it is plain to any reader of common sense that the ideas about the deepest truths of religion were practically the same in the language of Moses as they were in that of David and the other psalmists. It is also true that the greatest sages of our history, who have taught many things about ritual and other matters which do not appear to everybody to coincide in all their details with biblical teaching, have yet expressed about the Presence of God precisely the same teaching and the same aspirations upon which the earliest Judaism took its stand. Popular notions of spiritual life may vary, and popular conceptions both within and without the fold of Israel do vary.

But when we want to inquire what the Jewish teaching is upon those subjects, which after all constitute its inmost sanctuary, and we go to consult the records of Israel's masters and luminaries, we find absolute harmony. I believe that even in our own day, widely different as the outward religious practices of Jews undoubtedly are, you will find that all really religious Israelites feel exactly the same kind of hunger and thirst after the Presence of God, and the same assurance of rest in the attainment of that object. They may differ ever so much about their traditions on most subjects, and on the interpretation of Scripture, or even on the comparative authority of different parts of the Bible, but if they are in their heart of hearts true to the mission of their race, they will each and all recognize in such words as I have quoted the very soul of their ancestral faith. Of course, one might be told that many people have never become aware of the fact that their religion means anything at all except ritual and sanitary arrangements and racial ties, but such persons one is justified in describing, not necessarily reproachfully, but very certainly, as being misinformed about the true genius of Judaism. The human mind often finds it difficult to grasp at one and the same time a great many aspects of the same subject, and there can be little doubt that the elaborate network of ritual detail which has gathered around our historic Religion has in many cases induced a tendency, by no means anticipated by those who helped to erect it, to divert the thoughts from the deepest truths themselves and to fix them upon the fence which was intended to safeguard those truths. This consideration, however, is one which opens up a wide field of reflection to which I do not propose to invite your attention in this place. That intense desire on the part of Moses to enjoy the assurance of having with him the Presence of God; and that equally earnest passionate prayer of David entreating that he might not be cast away from the same Divine presence, exhibit a frame of mind, a condition of heart from which, I would submit, you and I of this 19th century ought to learn a very great truth. Either we have faith in God, or we have not. Is that faith, that Jewish faith, in which we often pride ourselves, a reality or only a dream? Is it possible really to have the Presence of God with us each personally, individually, or are we in uttering the words only expressing a wild imagination? People say they believe in God, they are sure that His righteousness exceeds anything it is possible to imagine; but they fail to appreciate or even to take account of that wondrous privilege inherent in human nature by which we are able in this busy world to live with Him. Men and women of the world, who seem to have their portion in this life, would make believe that they are quite independent of spiritual culture, but they are very weak mortals, indeed, who fight shy of preserving through life, the consciousness of the infinitely righteous Being. The mere contact with such a Presence must of necessity light up all the dark corners of our secret lives, and render glaring to our own perception some of those evils which perhaps we would rather had remained hidden. In the long run there is no complete assurance of rest without the tranquil conscience. For those even who imagine that they can find some substitute for God there is no unrest so disturbing as that by which they are out of harmony with their own natures. Of all kinds of unrest, there is none so exhausting as an inward turmoil of any sort, and of all inward turmoils what can be so disturbing as self discontent. The discontent which does not arise from the consciousness of actual sin, but rather from the disquieting moods of an unhappy disposition, must itself be trying to bear. And it is easy to understand how it is that people of this description shrink from admitting into their inner lives a condition which is liable to make manifest, though it does not create, actual causes of discontent. Faith of this high order, that is an intense desire for the abiding Presence of God, is surely the very substance of that message with which our race has been so singularly gifted, and which it is our peculiar mission to propagate.

Do we at all estimate what that faith actually means? It is one of those things which cannot be and which never was intended to be demonstrated in the nature of a mathematical proposition. Almighty God, who is surely our Father, or else we are not concerned with Him, has mystically determined that He shall become manifest to us through the feelings, through the affections, through a divine untold love. That is why the head corner-stone of Judaism is the command to love God with all the powers of our being. Love is the channel which He seems to have selected, and experience plainly declares that it is the only channel through which human life can be in living conscious touch with the divine. Without the incomparable power of love God cannot be realised in this world. No purely intellectual method of reasoning can translate for us the idea of the Presence of God from an abstract proposition into a vital virtue-propelling, conscious force. And this is just what we want to do with it. However industriously men of learning may pursue the study of Biblical literature and criticism, they will never quite experience that frame of mind which Moses enjoyed, and for which David petitioned, until they put forth the whole and undivided ardour of their affections.

Everybody knows what love means in some form or other. And human nature, by its special constitution, has ample faculty for exercising and receiving it. Human happiness, in the most ordinary sense, may be measured in every case by the quality and the degree of the special power to love and to be loved. That is the first condition of true happiness, and it is the only condition of the highest kind of happiness. No human being can for a single day enjoy happiness unless he loves and is loved. We all have various experiences of the human aspect of this divine gift of love. And we must know from observation, if happily not from experience, that the very essence of human misery is to be seen under the shadow of hate, enmity, and discord of all kinds. Civilization, that great word about which one hears and reads so much nowadays, is a condition which will grow only with the fading away of hostilities, and the rising of human love. Heaven on earth is well known to be found in a true domestic life. The love of kinsmen and of friends, whether in social intercourse, or only in silent memory, is the one strong foundation of human happiness, which the world and death itself cannot hinder. What then of that spiritual love which links us with the undying, the eternal, the perfectly righteous God? Shall not that be possible, when the very shadow of it in human affection is quite apparent? Such a love, and such a union are doubtless what these two great heroes of our race meant by asking that God's Presence should go with them. Why shall not we pray that prayer every day of our lives? If not for such an immediate purpose as that which caused the great legislator to seek it on the special occasion referred to in the text, at least may we not ask as much as the psalmist sought, by imploring that we may not be cast away from His presence, that He may not take from us His holy spirit? The greatest reform that we could effect in this generation would be to revive the spirit of those Israelites who were the authors of the Psalms and of the Books of the Prophets.

Indeed, revival must come in this age. People speak vaguely about the efficacy of prayer, as though it were a mere selfish, worldly method of getting material things, and it is invariably noticeable that these discussions miss the main issue of the question. Prayer—that is, conscious communion with our Eternal Father—is efficacious by reason of its potency to bring us into that true realised relation with Him, of which we are too long apt to remain practically unconscious. And think what it signifies in the very act of prayer, to take ourselves away from the crowded, busy, often unkind world, into that peaceful, tender, loving Presence of the Supreme Being, who does not weary. But by never being cast away from God's Presence, and having always His spirit with us, a vast deal more is meant than anything which is understood by a single act of worship. It is a life of worship, it is a life of peace, a life of rest, a life of steady adherence to fixed principles, and devotion to that kind of duty, and that estimate of duty which the common social standard does not of itself present. We heard two weeks ago in this place something about an ideal life, and how it was possible for everybody in any situation of life to live an ideal one. Just think of that secret power, the abiding Divine Presence, as the means to that end, if it be not in itself the end. A man who has always God before him, not in the sense of being unknown to himself, watched, scrutinised, and judged by an unseen eye, but living and acting in harmony, in conscious co-operation with that Divine Will, never revolting, always seeking to obey—is not that an ideal life? Some of you will say, that is an almost impossible picture, hardly an attainable goal. Tell us something easier to do, more within the reach of ordinary persons! The answer is that life is made up of such an innumerable quantity of details, and of little things, that there is only one way of equipping the human character, so that it can adapt itself to details of conduct in a way which would approach to an ideal life. That is by the application of one simple and uncomplicated habit of thought, a temper of mind, an attitude of the soul, one whole and complete spiritual equipment, and this is expressed by the desire to live with God. Then you will say that persons who profess to live with God, and who do so live are liable to error—David himself sinned. Quite true! But with this confession of the frailty and the weakness of human nature—for you would never declare that the man without God was really better off—is it not transparently plain that by not denying from oneself the presence of God, sin will be more easily detected and more speedily diminished if you would not admit that it was indeed more easily avoided. A man who lives with God is not constantly battling with sin. Human nature is just as capable of becoming averse to sin, as it is of acquiring an aptitude for sin. With the progress of spiritual culture vice in its grosser manifestation does not even appear in the form of temptations. Dishonesty, uncharity, impurity, become not merely conquered, but there is no effort at avoiding them. They present no kind of attraction. It is extremely difficult to depict the man whose life is distinguished by the realisation of the Divine Presence, but there are such persons. And if human history had presented no more than a single example of the kind, we should be logically justified in asserting that such a life is possible. But, happily, history abounds with types of men and women who have lived with God, and who have not encountered any sharp temptation to sin. Every generation, almost every family, has its record of the saintly mother, the angel sister, the sweet God-like child. And, thank God, we of the race of Israel have no cause to deplore the absence of such bright stars of human excellence. It is a degraded, an unnatural view of human destiny, which regards the main course of life as one dreary road to wickedness. It is a diseased condition of mind, a heathen conception, which has so grievously impressed upon multitudes the grim teaching that man is essentially vile. Judaism is a powerful protest through the ages against this unhealthy, morbid dictum. Men and women often make the mistake of forming their estimate of human character from what they read in the newspapers. The detection of crime and the revelation of vice do come to the surface, and modern journalism seems to delight in purveying with needless elaboration the worst that can be known of human nature. But against the sickening roll of sin laid before us day by day by the printing press, is there no balancing-sheet with its statement of human virtue? The exercise of a little imagination will discover, if we have not the opportunity of seeing through a wide experience of our fellows, a vast army of high-souled men and women of all ages and conditions spread broadcast through our great cities, among thousands of villages and in millions of homes, literally living with God and for God, carrying along with them the very touch of His holy spirit which acts possibly as the central light illuminating these unknown numbers of human circles. We can see it in the sturdy, manly nature of the perfect husband, the devoted father, who really goes through life with the single purpose to do his best for his family, possibly, against severe difficulties and acute anxieties, maintaining the freshness of youth through a long life, by reason of his own inward glow of the Divine presence. We can discover it in the gentle mother whose efforts in life amount to one long stride of self-negation. Outside the domestic sphere we find self-sacrifice, humility of spirit, tender care for others in every walk of life, from the high-minded statesman and the plodding scientist, to cheerful, kind-hearted hospital nurse, whose whole career means unselfishness. These are the public-spirited leaders and followers in a variety of movements designed for the alleviation of human suffering, or for the promotion of human welfare in a thousand different directions. Then there is that most luminous of all virtues, the widespread effort among hosts of men and women to save and to rescue from danger and temptation those who are deprived of their natural guardianship, or who, from personal infirmity of some kind, are constitutionally unable to protect their own lives. If it be true, and it is a fact, that London presents a vast spectacle of appalling wickedness, it is equally true that there is a preponderating balance of persons whose lives shine radiantly with the light of the Divine Spirit. Just consider the one trait in human character becoming, we rejoice to think, signally developed in the present generation, that of large-hearted charity. Perhaps its minor expression is in the giving of alms; but by far its weightier and more characteristic effect is seen in the power of withholding unkind judgment, of helping those who have fallen, in strengthening the weak, in countless tokens of intellectual and spiritual sympathy. The category of virtues is too long to enumerate, is too abundant in its manifestations to be detailed. It means not so much a number of excellent qualities as it does one whole condition of the heart and of the intellect. That condition, my friends, is secured in a life which seeks God for its mainstay.

The poet, Browning, has sung of such a life in these lines—

> This, throws himself on God the unperplexed,
> Seeking shall find him.

Which of us is not capable of making the effort to seek, of wending our way towards God? I would never believe that there is a Jewish man or woman or child who has not, deep, deep dow in his or her nature, the resources with which to commence, at least, the true spiritual culture.

After all there is an inalienable right of the human soul to have God with it in conscious relationship. Our race has taught this truth; and shall we, the teachers, forget what we have imparted? If there were not this inalienable right, there would be no meaning for us in all those attributes of our Divine Creator, which are so familiar in our prayers and in our praises which we offer to Him. The worship of God is the declaration on our part of that inalienable right. But what David asked, and what, I would submit, it is urgent that we should ask, is that that relationship with Him should hold good at all times and in all conditions of life. Otherwise, He, whom we describe in our liturgy as the great, mighty and tremendous God, would be away from ourselves, and His greatness, His might, and His power would only remotely interest us as though they were no more than the attributes of a powerful distant despot, far off and out of reach from all that is human. It is just this relation, this kinship, this tie, between the frail and sorrow-bearing mortal, and the Divine, unseen majesty which invests our species with its lofty nature, and endows us with an exalted yet possible aspiration. Such an aspiration is only natural to everyone who is created in the image of God. Let us, then, in no wise suppress the rising of this hope, but rather endeavour to nurture it that it may grow and strengthen. And let us consider that in every conscious effort towards the ideal life we are raising ourselves into the Divine Presence; that by each act of self-control, and by every attempt to subject the animal nature to nobler claims, we are clinging again and again to the Spirit of God, so that it shall not forsake us. There is no situation in ordinary life which may not be turned to such a use. Indeed, the methods are simple enough. What is primarily wanted is the will, the desire to let the Divine Presence go with us. Let us do nothing, and think nothing which we would screen from the Infinite eye. In every movement and turn of life—be the course ever so rugged or full of care—let us be quite sure that we are glad He is present to guide or to admonish. And, then, may we not hope that every step and that each act will be illumined by the light of the Divine Spirit.

HIGHER JUDAISM.

[*Kilburn, March* 19*th*, 1892.]

"Thy Kingdom is an everlasting Kingdom, and thy dominion endureth throughout all generations."—*Psalm* cxlv.

THIS is a very familiar psalm. So familiar indeed that, like other beautiful things that are constantly repeated, and frequently gabbled, it has almost lost its meaning to modern Jews. We may have noticed it among a host of other psalms that are included in the Liturgy of the synagogue, and there is none more commonly used than this one. These psalms are so crowded together, and so rapidly recited in the sacred language, that perhaps there are not a great many Jews or Jewesses on whom they make a very profound impression. "Familiarity breeds contempt" is a saying true enough in regard to a number of things, but it is nowhere more true than in connection with the lofty faith that is expressed again and again in the wonderful literature of our race. I never take up the Psalms, or indeed any edition of the Jewish Prayer Book, without a sense of the immense distance between the spiritual conception in the Jewish religion and the actual present day tone of our own people. The greatest reform of which we could conceive would be to raise the spiritual character of the present generation to the high level of the ancient psalmists of Israel. There is no greater anomaly than the fact that kinsmen of a race that is gifted above all other races in spiritual genius appear to be the least spiritual, and in many instances positively materialistic. Nor do we find that the spiritual life in the Jewish community is at all to be measured by the degrees of religious observance. Those who may be considered high authorities of what is called "orthodoxy" tell us that if we touch the ritualism of the most observant Jews we shall destroy their faith, for, say they, apart from those observances they have no faith at all. What greater proof can we have that so called religious observance and religion are two distinct things, which may or may not be combined? We in this place would be the last to deny that some of the most ardently spiritual natures, both in the present generation and in those that are gone, are to be found among some of the most observant Israelites. At the same time we also know that by far the larger proportion of those who are most particular as to ritual practices have no conception whatever of the spiritual hunger and thirst after God and righteousness. On the other hand it is most important that we here should not be unmindful of another consideration. There have arisen two unfortunate terms, known as "Orthodox" and "Reform," neither of which conveys any true representation of the spiritual character of the individual, or of the groups who are thus designated. And we may take it that in both cases the words are worth little more than signifying different standards or degrees of ceremonial practice. Many so-called "Reformers" understand by the expression nothing higher or nothing deeper than a change in the arrangements of public worship and in congregational management. Is it too bold to express the opinion that these terms as generally accepted are entirely conventional, and rather of a secular than of a sacred import? It may be, and it undoubtedly is the case that certain spiritual temperaments do crave after a system of public worship which must involve considerable change in the methods now in use; but let it be clearly observed that those changes, and changes there must be, are merely the external consequences and not the primary motive of a truly religious reform. If, for example, we discover from experience that our capacity for entering into communion with God at public worship is marred, and sometimes actually destroyed by forms that seem repugnant to us, we cannot and ought not to force ourselves to abide by those practices, and thus retard our spiritual progress. We must demand in such circumstances a different mode of public worship that shall be in accord with the necessities of our case. After all what is the aim of public worship if it be not to enable a number of persons congregated together to draw near unto God, and to acquire by means of that worship the blessings of an increased spiritual insight? Of course different people attend public worship for different reasons. Some do not go there for purposes of personal comfort and worship at all, but solely as an act of conformity to the custom of the community to which they belong, to testify by their presence a certain good fellowship, and an intention to co-operate with that community in the special works of charity that fall upon it. With such persons attendance at public worship is a kind of roll-call, by which their mere presence answers to their names in a registered list. To people of this description alterations in the manner of service are of no interest, and that being so, the avoidance of any fresh undertaking would be sufficient motive to make them resist rather than support any proposal for change. But with them I contend we have upon this particular subject no common ground, no logical basis of argument whatever, until we have succeeded in first altering their conception of the objects of synagogue attendance. With another class, however, I trust more numerous, of persons who do profess the same view of public worship that we do ourselves, we have a very exact and vital contention. Theoretically they confess with ourselves that the objects of public worship are entirely religious and personal, but many of them refuse to admit that existing methods do in reality frustrate those objects. Now, my friends, the realisation of a Divine Presence, and the acknowledgment of kinship between the individual soul and the Spirit of God, are unquestionably the aim of Divine worship. In other words, faith of the purest and of the highest character is what justifies us in making the efforts we do to purify the ritual, and to improve the method of teaching Judaism. The struggle which is now going on in our community, not in one district but everywhere, is the most encouraging symptom of a true religious revival. The discontent at things as they are, a discontent which can no longer be disguised, is a guarantee that Israel is not asleep in the presence of the everlasting kingdom of which she is the witness. These words that I have quoted are constantly at every service, I believe, in the mouth of the Israelite, and yet that kingdom which we are so frequently and, alas! so mechanically mentioning, is not to the present generation the reality that it ought to be. Is this fact due to a want of faith, or is it due to any defects in the prevailing methods of our religious teaching and of our worship? The answer comes that it is due to both these causes, the one reacting on the other. Increase of faith, and an improvement in the spiritual life of our community, are without doubt the most urgent needs at the present time. Upon that all the guides of our community are agreed, however widely they differ as to the means.

Stolid resistance to a genuine claim for alterations in our forms and observances does not seem to us to be the best solution of the difficulty. Experience is the greatest of all teachers, and we have the experience of many generations to support our contention that the religious apathy around us has not been averted by the maintenance of things as they were. If experience is to be the test of what is best calculated to promote a high spiritual life, then we may safely assert that so far experience is practically all on one side. Can any honest mind deny that the form of worship in ninety-nine synagogues out of a hundred is such as to repel rather than to arouse the devotional instinct? I was told the other day by a conscientious Israelite of the old school that the main purpose of public worship on the Sabbath morning was to listen to the reading of the Law, and that that function ought properly to occupy the major portion of time. Do we find then that the reading of the Law, as it is carried out in the vast majority of synagogues, has the effect of awakening a devout spirit, a spirit of drawing nigh unto God, one which arouses in the average Jewish soul feelings of sacred love and of holy resolve? The experience of most of us, even of those who express that view of Sabbath worship just mentioned, is the direct contrary. Ought we to blink this fact? Is it honest to do so? Are we by such a contention contributing one jot to the increase of faith and the improvement in our spiritual tone? Again, as to the manner of uttering the prayers, such prayers as the time left after the lengthy reading of the Law permits, are they offered in a way that seems to bring God's presence closer to us? How often have we experienced that the religious emotions which were aroused on entering a Jewish sanctuary before the service commenced and while it was empty, were almost magically suppressed as soon as the people assembled and the sacred office was begun. This question of remodelling the public worship of the synagogue has been too long delayed, and it is now the immediate question that must be presented to our community. It does not brook delay. No considerations of expediency can justify us in shelving that question for another generation, for, alas! one generation more may be too late. In all directions we must perceive, if we are candid, that a new generation of English Jews and Jewesses are growing up strangers to our ancient sanctuary, drifting slowly and in large numbers, perhaps irrevocably, from the fold of Israel. To defer this question means to acquiesce in this loss which is daily becoming more imminent to the Synagogue and to Judaism itself. If we could arise in a future generation and look back on the fallen sanctuary, would we do so with a tranquil conscience unless we had done our very utmost to save the Synagogue in the only way which our conscience had dictated? The duty of pressing upon our brethren at this present time the urgent claims of religious progress—and that involves ritual reconstruction—is so great, that we must not be terrified by any fears that are held out as to mere party divisions. If party divisions do arise in consequence of the determination of some of us to prosecute the work of religious progress, those divisions, harmful as they might be to Israel's cause, would be immeasurably less dangerous than the other course of preparing for a new generation in whom the blood of Israel alone can be traced, the faith gone, departed. But is it possible that we can be taunted with threatening divisions when our action is the sole outcome of our faith whic all Jews profess? Believing that God's kingdom is everlasting, that His dominion endureth from generation to generation, can we suppose that any effort to make this truth live in the hearts of our own generation, can destroy the very faith which we would thus resuscitate? Let there be parties by all means. Let one congregation vie with another in the proclamation of the deepest truths of our religion; better far than that they should be rivals in presenting a spectacle of spiritual destitution. Faith is what we proclaim. Religious faith alone can secure the permanence of Judaism. Faith is what is threatened by those who have lifted custom out of its place, and who would stem the tide of progress by raising precedent into a rank to which it has no claim. The movement of which these services are the embodiment fills a vacant gap, and is the first sign of religious revival for fifty years. It was never conceived in the spirit of party or of division. On the contrary, you have helped forward the religious aspirations of your neighbours whose methods differed from your own. May not one who can claim no share in your efforts express the hope that Almighty God may bless and help forward the work which you have begun, and that this work may spread in all directions where English Jews are found. This model Jewish service might be held in different districts of London, and thus present a lesson of what is meant by a solemn and reverent worship. There is one more consideration which I would urge for the extension of religious services such as these. Religion is a gift, faith is the faculty by which it is apprehended. That gift is locked up in the average Jewish soul, sometimes never unlocked. The consciousness of our kinship with the Creator of unknown worlds, and the hereditary trust to Jews of being His kingdom of priests and a holy nation, are truths of so spiritual a nature that they cannot be left to the influences of race merely. The best possibilities of human achievement, both in science and in moral excellence, confirm the testimony of the Divine Presence within us. But it is the personal and secret conviction treasured up in one soul after another, receiving constant renewal by prayer, that makes up the sum of human witness to our affinity with the living God. If this is a natural human faith, what must be its intensity in the mind of an Israelite? Some natures seem to be more endowed than others with the conviction of God's abiding presence, and less dependent, therefore, on external influences. Faith, love and sorrow are three elements that mysteriously blend in human experience, each having its own tale to tell of the relation which we bear to the Supreme Being. The faculty of faith, which brings God so close to us, and which helps us to understand our relation with that everlasting kingdom, is one of development. It is something to be nurtured in the child's soul when it is fresh and unsophisticated. It should always be associated in early life with what is tender, with what is sweet and happy, and never with what is bitter or gloomy. It cannot be well that it should fall under the weight of wearisome and unæsthetic ceremonial, or of long prayers that no child can understand. During the period of youth that mystical gift of faith, generally understood as the religious instinct, should be impressed by what is solemn and reverent, and for this reason it appears to be of primary consequence at the present time that all the religious influences of the Synagogue, such as public worship, should be of a kind to confirm and deepen those impressions, and not to nullify them. Throughout our personal career, especially after we have gained maturity, religion and faith will be essentially matters of experience and inward culture. The Divine Presence will be found in the imperishable sanctuary of our own higher natures, revealed to us in our own bitter moments of conscientious struggle and self-sacrifice, when we are fighting the battle against sin and selfishness, when we are wrestling with the temptations of the world in order to preserve the empire of truth and genuineness. The Divine revelation is found somewhere else as well as on the shelves of a library or in the ark of the Synagogue. We seem to meet God face to face—even as the first teacher of Israel had met Him—at times of conflict with our own natures, when we are striving to give the victory to the truth and the purity of which we are not wholly unpossessed, and when we are called upon in a moment to choose between good and evil. Sometimes the choice appears in the form of personal integrity against the possession of wealth, or even the surrender of some favourite pursuit or acquaintance as the alternative of doing violence to our conscience. These struggles are much more frequent than we are apt to suppose. When they come we are not always ready to let in the blazing light of the Divine kingdom. For the teaching of this higher Judaism much change is required in the methods which now prevail.

RELIGIOUS CALM.

[*Manchester Reform Synagogue, July 2nd,* 1892.]

"For thus saith the Lord God, the Holy One of Israel: In returning and rest shall ye be saved; in quietness and confidence shall be your strength."—*Isaiah* xxx. 15.

THE present generation, which is remarkable for a splendid development in many directions, is yet hindered by certain evils. Previous generations have had their evils too, some of them of a grosser kind than those which specially belong to our own time. It is well that each generation should be aware of its weaknesses, in order that danger may be arrested by the exercise of restraint. We do not live in an age of sloth. If it be true that luxury and self-indulgence prevail very much, they are of a kind quite different from what they were in that generation which preceded the French Revolution. The luxury and indulgence of the present day, like most other things, is attended by an enormous expenditure of energy and labour. It is not perhaps on that account less mischievous than when it assumed the form of lassitude and sloth. People who are bent on a life of selfish enjoyment have certainly nowadays to exert themselves in pursuit of it. Distances must be traversed, sleepless nights must be endured, and a good deal of personal discomfort has to be encountered, in order to enjoy to any large extent what are called the worldly pleasures of this age. With such activity there may be as much moral indolence as in the days of lounging and feasting, but from the different circumstances of this generation there can scarcely be the same mental or physical inertia.

If we consider the condition of our own time, excluding from view the self-indulgent portion of our fellows, we fail to discover in any walk of life the idleness and inactivity which have marked certain periods of history. On the contrary, there is probably no feature of this age more striking than its extraordinary activity and general movement. Indeed the experience which is presented to us who reside in a vast and overgrown metropolis must be anything but that of quietness and rest. In every department of industry there appears to be a hurry and a rush. The intense competition in the professions and in commerce, leaves no chance for the innumerable band of bread-seekers to take things easily. To the vast majority of Londoners, the difficulty of earning a livelihood appears to have increased to an almost alarming degree. When we consider that for every vacant situation, no matter of what kind, there is a crowd of applicants, most of them probably equally competent, and if we realise that the most ordinary situation makes a claim upon its aspirant, which signifies that he must produce a very full, a very careful measure of work indeed for the wage he desires to earn, we come to perceive the high pressure of City daily life. No doubt the spread of national education within the last twenty years has very much tended to increase the expectations and the demands of all sorts of employers of labour.

The fierceness of the struggle, and the keenness of the competition, even for daily bread, not to mention more ambitious aims, do at times appear to convert our population into something like a warfaring multitude, fighting for their very existence. In these circumstances, the present generation is characterised by a serious tendency to unrest. Many years ago, one of the greatest men of the nineteenth century, described the lives of the poorest sections of English society as " one ghastly procession of hungry millions, from the cradle to the grave." It is impossible to resist the reflection that so much over-work, over-crowding together, with the physical consequences of such conditions, must in time affect, if they have not already affected, the moral and the spiritual constitution of our generation. Those of us who are not directly affected by the undue competition for subsistence, or the overstrain of too much work must in the long run be touched, more or less, by the tendency of the age.

Let us see how this tendency of unrest and disquietude enters into the sphere of religion, and indeed, let us reflect how religion may come to our rescue, and mitigate the evils arising from such circumstances. First we stand in great need in the present generation of saving religion itself from the consequences of permitting it to be drawn into the circle of those many subjects in respect to which turmoil rather than peace prevails. The general movement of our time in its intellectual aspect has so far brought about more good than harm. Scientific research has received a valuable impetus in the present generation. Literature and art have both been visibly affected by the general intellectual progress. And if in either of those fields there is not quite the same proportion of genius which have adorned other generations, yet they are both more systematically taught and more methodically pursued. This is the natural result of an improved method of education. Religion, the rock of ages, is called upon to answer in this generation to the special cry which we make to it. The discussion of religious subjects is an inevitable part of the general exercise of our inquiring faculties, to which by the conditions of our time we are singularly impelled. But let not our lives be too much absorbed in the mere discussion of something which after all is to be our actual mainstay. It is no more possible to make all men and women think exactly alike about the various matters with which religion is connected than it is with any other matters with which some other vital interest is bound. Do not let us be so much absorbed with questions which after all only touch the fringe of the religious idea, while our days and our years are consumed and the deepest truths themselves remain obscured. It is much to be feared that Jews and Jewesses, like other people, loiter about a good deal around the outer Courts of their temple, where they conduct their unceasing disputations, while they never permit themselves to look at the inmost sanctuary itself. Now in these days of hurry and scurry, when the value of time and the brevity of life seem more formidable than they ever did before, there is an urgent necessity to treasure up what is precious in our own inmost sanctuary. The peace of God is no empty phrase, and such expressions as those with which our psalmists and our prophets have made us familiar have for us of this particular generation a significance which we cannot too highly prize.

"Thou will keep him in perfect peace whose mind is stayed on thee, because he trusteth in thee,' are words which have an inestimable value for everybody now just as they had for the author of the 26th chapter of Isaiah, who was evidently recording his personal experience when he wrote them.

Again, "Lead me to the rock which is higher than I." "For with thee is the fountain of life, in thy light shall we see light." Such expressions as these convey to us something of the personal experience and feeling of Israelites who knew a great deal more about the inmost sanctuary of Judaism than many of our partisans and controversialists. For people constituted like ourselves, active and energetic in the ordinary affairs of life, people who are liable to become constantly weary and careworn, the ancient Hebrew faith in God must be of inestimable value. It is exceedingly probable that the great luminaries of our faith, such persons as those who were the authors of the book of Psalms and the wonderful body of literature known as the books of the prophets, troubled their minds very much less than we do about such details as the hour for commencing public worship, the particular mode of conducting it, whether this paragraph or that should be recited. The greatest reform that we could effect in this generation would be to revive the spirit of some of these men. The conscious communion with the living God resorted to habitually would help us to assimilate that true Religious life.. It would be a wonderful rest for our exhausted souls. It would be a refreshing change to rush away for a moment from the busy unkind world to that peaceful, tender, loving presence of the Supreme Being who is never weary. Oh that we could keep alive in this generation that ancient faith! Do we at all estimate what it really means. It is one of those things which cannot be and which never was intended to be demonstrated in the nature of a mathematical proposition. Almighty God, who is surely our Father, or else we are not concerned with Him, has mystically determined that He shall become manifest to us through the affections, through the feelings, through a divine untold love.

Rest and quiet are two things about which people hold very different views. What is rest to one man might be considered monotony to another. So too with regard to recreation generally. Recreation really means a revivifying influence of some sort; some people's recreation would be actual work to others. But we all need it in some form.

"There is a danger in many cases of this need being overlooked. Let us understand the exact kind of rest which is particularly needful, and which is not always included in the popular notions. Everybody is aware of that kind of rest which is called physical; cessation of work, and sleep itself are universally admitted to be indispensable. But there is another kind of rest which may be enjoyed simultaneously with the daily exercise of our working faculties. This is an inward composure, a calm self-possession, a steady adherence to fixed principles. The busy man of the world might acquire it, and is certainly more in need of it than the hermit or recluse. It is a sort of composure which is quite compatible with outward activity and mental activity too. The increase of work rather suggests the desirability of such inward composure. Some people suffer from a constitutional state of excitability. They endure an amount of inward irritation and internal worry which is almost destructive of other noble qualities. We have all come in contact with persons who never seem to enjoy much presence of mind. They are impetuous, always hasty, seldom quiet, and when called upon to make a sudden decision in some moment of emergency, they seem to lose the ordinary sense with which every intelligent human being is really endowed. This condition entails a constant wear and tear of the spirit, and in time works a deleterious impression on the bodily health. How many people suffer from sleepless nights, mainly in consequence of an ill-regulated habit of thought? How much more easily we could get through the vicissitudes of this earthly career—so full of care and anxieties to many of us, in some respect or another a battle for everybody—if only we could preserve the calm inward self. One of the peculiar functions of religion is surely that it shall lead the human soul to a more serene and, indeed, to a healthier daily life than most other agencies can do. It is perfectly natural that we should look to religion to do for us what no other power is capable of achieving. People sometimes discuss what they call the efficacy of prayer, and it is invariably noticeable that somehow or other such discussion misses rather the main issue of the question. Prayer, that is, conscious communion with our eternal Father, is mainly efficacious by reason of its power of bringing us into that actual realised relation with Him of which we are too long apt to remain practically unconscious. People say they believe in God, they are sure that He is the most perfect being it is possible to imagine; but they fail somewhat to appreciate or even to take account of that wondrous privilege inherent in human nature, namely, that it is possible for us, even in the busy world, to live with Him. In this generation there is especial need of making the Supreme Being a greater reality for us. We stand rather more in need of strengthening our spiritual aspirations than we do of conforming to outward observances. We need not abandon outward observances, for with some temperaments they are calculated to induce a high spiritual culture. But what we want is God himself, with all the inward rest and peace which His vivifying presence can alone secure. Men and women of the world, who seem to have their portion in this life, would make believe that they are quite independent of spiritual culture; but they are very weak mortals indeed who fight shy of preserving through life the consciousness of the infinitely righteous God. The mere contact with such a presence is likely to light up all the dark corners of our secret lives, and to render glaring to our own perception some of those evils to which we would rather have remained blindfold. In the long run there is no complete assurance of quietness and confidence without the tranquil conscience.

Even for those who imagine they can find some substitute for God, there is no unrest so disturbing as that by which they are out of harmony with their own natures. Of all kinds of unrest there is none so exhausting as an inward turmoil of any kind; and of all inward turmoils, what can be so disturbing as self-condemnation? Even that discontent which does not arise from the consciousness of actual sin, but rather from the disquieting mood of a discontented disposition, must be in itself trying to bear; but what is known as a discontented disposition is not possible with a person who is really conscious of the abiding presence of God. The fact that there are so many persons of discontented disposition who are not disbelievers in the Supreme Being, shows how inadequately religion has presented itself to their minds, and how much of the vital issues in religion have been really missed. The construction of character is, after all, the avowed object of all religious organisations. We, Jews and Jewesses, think that there is not one more capable of effecting that object than our own. We are entitled to think so, and if we thought otherwise it would be hypocrisy to remain Jews and Jewesses. The luminaries of our faith, our prophets, and, no doubt, the greatest of our sages, too, laid enormous stress on this particular function of Judaism. Do not let us of this generation relax and emphasise some other object less transcendent in import.

> In returning and rest shall we be saved,
> In quietness and confidence will be our strength.

THE LIBERTY OF THE SOUL.

An Unspoken Sermon for the Feast of Passover.

והיהלך לאות על־ידך ולזכרון בין עיניך למען תהיה תורת יי בפיך :

"And it shall be for a sign unto thee upon thine hand, and for a memorial between thine eyes, that the Lord's law may be in thy mouth."—*Exodus* xiii. 9.

THIS quotation from the sacred records of the Exodus from Egypt fitly describes the object of the celebration of the Passover. The festival of emancipation has for us who commemorate it at this distance of time, a significance beyond the considerations of family and race. We are preserving the memory of an event which has a deep ethical meaning. We will endeavour to examine it and turn it to a practical and personal use.

The liberty of the soul is the best type of all freedom. The deliverance from the bondage which enslaves many a soul is a thought that should enter our hearts now. Looking back into the past, we see what that Passover did for Israel, and what it has done for mankind. If it had been no more than the liberation of a band of serfs, we should recognise a victory for the cause of freedom; and we might indeed wonder why that particular liberation should be so marked in its anniversaries thousands of years afterwards. It was a liberation, under Divine Providence, for a great purpose, far-reaching in influence, and wide-spreading in relation to the vast masses of people outside the small emancipated group. It is natural, indeed, my brethren, that at each annual commemoration we should be disposed to look back and to look forward. The past has its great lessons and its hallowing inspiration for those who are bound to it by ties of kinship and self-sacrifice. But the subject of our reflections does not end here. We cannot help looking into the future, and dwelling with something like enthusiasm upon the part we have to play in it, the responsibilities which devolve on us as the "Kingdom of Priests," the "witnesses."

The Exodus from Egypt was but a preparatory movement. It was a trial of strength, a test of endurance, but, what is of greater moment, it was a consolidation of forces. The ultimate object was neither military nor political. It was a moral expedition. Our ancestors were sent into the world to proclaim the law of righteousness, and to teach men God. The leaders were gifted with a spiritual insight which was unknown at the time, and were charged with the mission of infusing it into their kinsmen, thus preparing them to become the missionaries to the world. The genius of moral perception and of religious thought was theirs, their distinctive characteristic. Other groups of people had their special missions allotted to them. Was there any more sacred or so necessary to the happiness of mankind? The charms of literature and art are less essential to the happiness of the human soul than the tranquil conscience, the calm inward self which religion can prepare. How far we have executed our work up to the present time is not easy to estimate with accuracy, because we all have to admit that there was at various periods of our history, a falling-off from duty; and we have not in all the ages risen to the grandeur of our charge; we have constantly been rebuked for our sluggishness. This was only to be expected, because we were human, and we had a mighty task to emancipate our souls from the temptations of the world and of sin. Yet for all this there has been a vast spreading of Divine Truth through the instrumentality of our Race. After the Exodus from Egypt we were permitted to produce a literature, which has become the Bible of vast portions of the civilized world. Our prophets, our wise men, our warriors have spread their spiritual life in all directions. They are looked up to, their words are treasured, their examples are held sacred by millions of men who have never personally seen a single Jew. So tremendous has been the moral victory of our race, that multitudes of people are at this time worshipping the God whom we taught them, while they are scarcely conscious of the name of their teachers. The most devout lives in Europe, the most loving disciples of the law of God, have gained what they enjoy of those blessings, directly or indirectly, from the voice and teaching of Israel. Some recognise it; some are ignorant of it; the majority are in the position of those who are, as helpless infants, unable to realise who it is that is administering to their wants. Let it be so. For the spiritual benefactor requires no human recognition; his work is of God.

The vicissitudes of our people, so sore and full of sorrow, were, in a deep sense, a powerful training for those whose mission was moral. They were of the nature of that "refining" of which the Psalmist wrote. "As silver is tried in a furnace," so have been the great men of Israel sanctified by suffering. And they have presented to the world a model of those virtues which are only developed in suffering —endurance and courage, resolution and hope. There have been times in our history when to remain in the covenant required the heart of a saint and the patience of a martyr. And even in epochs in which the stake and the flames were no longer to be feared, there was yet the endurance under religious, social and political oppression. In the first part of this century in our own beloved England, it required a great spirit to remain faithful under the disabilities, and in spite of the temptation to desert our post. This is shown clearly by the fact that those who had not sufficient heroism to face the struggle did desert it, and yielded to the allurements of free citizenship. Those who remained—happily the great majority, —proved that they were not wanting in that heroic character which has so constantly been demanded from Israelites.

There are times of ease and luxury which have followed periods of privation and misery. It is remarkable, however, that in examining the state of Israel throughout the world, we can never cite a period since the dispersion when ease and luxury were universal. They have been, so far, invariably partial. At the present time we are experiencing the illustration of this assertion. We are free and at ease in England, in France, America, and elsewhere; but we are heavily laden in Russia, in Roumania, and Morocco. But, trusting as we are bound to do in the Divine law of progress, we believe that all will in the end come right. Those of us who are at ease have the active work, imperative upon us, of hasting to the rescue of others, as well as of seeing to our own development. We have no plea against the duty of ordering our efforts with a view to a greater future in the spreading of religious truth. This Passover is no time of wailing in England or in France, but of pure rejoicing. "Rejoice with trembling!" We must tremble with the sense of the heavy responsibilities which are upon us, for ourselves, for our brethren, for our Divine Cause. We are called upon to succour the unfortunate, to heighten our own spiritual condition, and to exhibit to the world in brighter lustre than ever the lights which we have. In this age of materialism and anarchy, a people whose sole mission is moral enlightenment have a great part to perform, an example to set of the reverse of those evils which beset society. We have the pure worship of a Perfect God; we possess a code of unassailable morals. Charity in its highest form is the watchword of Judaism. The love of God is the basis of action in Jewish life; the love of our neighbour is the reflection of the love of God. Here at once is the great banner of civilisation, the very ideal of the most earnest philanthropist. That cosmopolitanism which is expressed in the phrase, Common Fatherhood of God and Universal Brotherhood of men, is ours. It was revealed to our ancestors. We have suffered for centuries upon centuries to preserve it, and to keep it unaltered by the complication of more recent creeds. It is ours to make the best use of it for the benefit of our fellow-men beyond and outside the synagogue. What has anarchy to say to this? Rebellion is dumbfounded, order is sanctified. Brother Israelites! do not let us mistake our calling; do not let us suppose for a moment that we are banded together for any purpose except to be the teachers and exemplars of that Divine and civilising truth. No one shall say of us, "These people are exclusive, they keep themselves apart." We keep ourselves distinct, but not apart. To be apart implies a social separateness, but to be distinct means to live for a distinct purpose; and our distinct purpose is to teach men union, to break down barriers by moral exertion, and to show all men of every sect and place this common object. What is implied by the love of neighbour, as the reflex of the love of God, is a truth which sinks deeply into personal and practical use, as we observed at the outset, for where there is this love there is perfect freedom. The human soul is elevated from the snares of the world and the flesh, which so much burden it and impede its culture. The human soul, to fulfil its immortal destiny, requires very great room, it needs breadth of action, it is ever sighing for more and more liberty. Its destiny being eternal, and godlike in its object, it cannot have too much liberty. Again, human souls are so different one from another. Let it be understood that in speaking of human souls we mean the higher self, that part of us which is distinct from the animal life. It embraces the intellect, or rather the intellect is one of its expressions. We have said that human souls are so different: that is, that the variety of temperaments and dispositions is so great in human nature that it is impossible to lay down in detail a system of life and thought which will suit every one. The attempt to do it, so often tried, is opposed to this divine principle of liberty which we are commemorating. Thanks be to God that in our grand religion this necessary freedom is so well recognised. The Mosaic legislation, when it goes into details, is providing mainly for the externals of society. When it touches upon purely spiritual themes, there is at once free scope. All we can do with one another is to recommend, in fraternal love, what we honestly conceive to be the best guarantee for happiness—a happiness which the world cannot assail, because it founds itself not on the things of this world, or upon any transient condition. It is founded upon an inward personal construction of character. There can be this construction within—a Kingdom of Heaven planted there—a state of mind constituted, which has for its goal the establishment of useful ideas, wide culture, large imagination, that can take into its grasp conditions differing from it. These are objects which no mundane circumstance can stop; the pursuit of them must be a perpetual source of happiness, ever increasing with refreshing vigour, and ultimately gaining the victory over all ill, and even conquering death. This is the true liberty of the soul. These are the reflections which this greatest festival of liberty suggests. The voice of our prophet speaks to us: "Break forth into joy, for the Lord hath comforted His people, and all the ends of the earth shall see the salvation of our God."

INTROSPECTION.

An Unspoken Sermon.

"O let me not wander from Thy Commandments."—*Psalm* cxix. 10.

THERE is a touch of deep pathos in this prayer—so human and so descriptive, that it seems to present a picture of the suppliant. Considering the words in connection with those immediately before them—"With my whole heart have I sought Thee"—they show the character of a man who is fully serious and right-minded in his intentions, and who is conscious of his weakness; of one who is convinced that a life of righteousness is the life worth living, but realises from experience the enormous difficulties in attaining it. He appreciates the fact that there is a distance between right views of life and the actual living rightly. The consideration of such a character is our present object.

It must be within the observation of any one who has studied human life, that a well intentioned person is often anxious to dissociate himself from religious beliefs, because people who profess them do not appear in his judgment the better for them.

The seeming force of this objection disappears upon examination. They who make it do not justly measure the proportions between human feeling and human conduct. They assume that there must be an immediate outward verification of a man's views, which would be wonderful when the facts of progress and struggle are taken into account. They do not recognise that he who has a great ideal and exalted views is yet like themselves, feeble in will, and exposed to more or less the same temptations: moreover, that the very presence of his ideal and his exalted views gives him a longer race to run, and greater heights to ascend; and that the frequent sense to him of his distance from his destination, brings with it an amount of inward depression, which often retards him. Temperament is so strange, that when a man is disheartened enough to give up the moral race which he has set himself, his mind still clings to the ideas that started the race, and then we have what is called, or seems to be, a hypocrite. Of course it must be admitted that hypocrisy as understood by the world is dangerous to the cause of religious teaching, and in bringing odium upon the name of religion, the guilty one is thoroughly mischievous. It is, therefore, of transcendent importance that there should be some safeguard against this danger, not only to protect the man from the sin or appearance of hypocrisy, but, also, to save to religious teaching its power for good. With these views we can understand the apprehension and tenor of the writer of the Psalms, who has, in his own confession, "sought with his whole heart," which made him say, " O let me not wander from Thy Commandments." Here was a great spiritual character, keen, ardent, and longing after righteousness, a man, whose views of life and conduct were part of his own temperament, who was anxious to make others share his convictions, a man whose earnestness could not be doubted. He knew and understood human nature probably better than any one of his time, and there was no one who came more in contact with men—he was thoroughly human. His life was by no means a perfect example, and he had the dreadful fear that he might possibly "wander." He evidently could see all the consequences of wandering, to himself, and to his great cause. As it is, there is a vulgar criticism of that life, which is willing to rob it of all its exalted teaching, because it fell short in itself.

It is quite clear that with or without religion there is an awful wandering away from perfect law; but let us consider here the wandering of those who have, at some time or other, known intimately the perfect law.

It ought to be impossible, one might think, for a person who has once known what perfect law is and recognised its binding claim, to wander from it. This may seem reasonable and natural; but it is not true, for such men do "wander." Well, how do they come to wander? If human nature were quite consistent, and every part of the man's being worked harmoniously, there would be no wandering. But this is not the case. We are bound to recognise that there are many opposing forces in human nature, and call them by any names we will, they exist, and they must be dealt with. There is the ill-balance of a mind which was even gifted, and there is overgrowth of one particular failing, which has been let almost unconsciously to make its strides, and in the end, wreck the whole man. With regard to the will, that is absolutely a matter of discipline, and only slow, regular, and constant effort can train it to become the servant of the manhood. This of itself is almost a lifelong work. If the will is anything except the actual servant of the man, we discover in it sufficient cause for all kinds of wandering in all manner of directions.

Then there is the reasoning with oneself, sometimes going wrong. A compromise takes place within between right and wrong, and the soul begins to "wander." We reason with ourselves unfairly, partially, favouring a particular impulse, without direct reference to the perfect law. If it were possible to obtain an experience of what goes on in the private thoughts of men and women, we might hear such sentences as these: "I might do worse," "This is not so bad as that," and there are apologies made to the conscience for a temporary breach of faith with it. All this is wandering, and, whilst at the time the guilt is scarcely discernible, when it is examined afterwards, under the microscope of that perfect law, it is conspicuous. Then there is the idea so plausible and so misleading, "I can't always be under that great microscope." This process of thought causes us to look at our conduct with other eyes than those of the perfect law. It would be a truism to mention the force of habit, and yet it is amazing to discover how a habit is contracted; from a slight circumstance that is easily forgotten, a habit of mind is gained which causes moral failure. A person who had always thought it wrong to condemn anybody, to judge his neighbour, after a lapse of time, is found to be in the constant habit of speaking against people, one of the most deadly forms of uncharity. That habit grew so gradually and imperceptibly, that he had not realised that he was wandering from perfect law. It is needless to illustrate what are known as the grosser habits, because they are glaring. It is enough, here, to consider the habits which society presents in a form that is thought quite respectable. They are called social failings, sometimes they are regarded as quite justifiable, but as a matter of fact they prove that there is wandering from perfect law. To judge an acquaintance with a rigour which it could not be supposed Divine mercy would entertain, is a distinct evil. To fail to recognise that claim for consideration, which is the first element in the mercy of God, is obviously ungodlike, and, therefore, wandering from perfect law. The indulgence of any propensity which is a source of discomfort to another is an act of selfishness. And, yet, persons who bear excellent characters keep those about them in constant turmoil, by a propensity which shows itself in cynicism or unpleasant temper; these are departing from perfect law. To the period of life called youth, it is clear, that the greatest danger is uncontrolled passion. This is an old story, as old as the hills but not less real. The idea is that in youth passion is more difficult to combat than in later life. This is a popular mistake; it can be conceived that in all cases of wandering, the time when it is most easy to arrest the wanderer is in the first stage. Then comes the difficulty, that experience, being the only means likely to convince a person of an evil, is naturally absent in youth. We must recognise this difficulty, and believe that to be the reason why youth is so little protected against sin. Not necessarily because its passion is stronger, but because experience is wanting. Now to supply the place of experience there must be principle, if for no other reason. In the presence of perfect law we cannot consent to any principle inferior and less potent. Well, where there has been that safeguard, the perfect law, there comes, if not always, very frequently, the wandering from it. The presence of the perfect law does not remove those opposing forces, nor does it alter the nature of the will. All this has still to be accomplished, the discipline must take place in its own course, which we have seen is slow, and the opposing forces have to be reconciled and regulated. All this is a tremendous work which no man can find easy. It is, however, infinitely more possible in the presence of perfect law than it would be without it. Then comes the necessity of retracing steps for him who has wandered. There is the going back to the point where the perfect law was left; this is possible, but difficult. Resolution is feeble because it is too often emotional, and as emotion is of a temporary nature, the poor resolution drops with it. There must be the principle of work in a human soul. The soul has to say to itself, "I have a given work to do, my will is out of training, I am not master of it"; and then there must take place a conscious exercise of the will, just as much as one consciously exercises a limb. That *will*, by steady working at it, must be made to do positive service. It has to acquire the power of resistance, the capability of saying to the impulses and passions, "you shall do this," or "you shall not do that." Such a course of effort may be considered a difficult ethical problem; the difficulty is not in the reasoning but in the doing it. Then, again, those opposing forces in human nature must harmonise.

That line between the spiritual life and the animal life has to be marked clearly enough, so that there shall be no confusion between spiritual intention and animal passion. Affections require careful training. Men and women have to analyse what they call "love" in order to see that they have in it the right proportion of unselfish purpose. With this training of the will, and harmonising of the different forces of our nature, we are building up a well-developed character. To accomplish that is surely a life's work, and the life that works at it is the life worth living. It is an ambition for the most ardent nature, and in labouring for it the work is unselfish and wide-spreading; and, therefore, in the ideal sense, it is benefiting humanity. With such a goal before an earnest spirit, how fearful and appalling must be the sense with which he must dread slipping away, wandering from the path; especially when he has sought it out with all his heart, how constantly he must pray the prayer, "O let me not wander from Thy commandments."

We have so far considered the difficulties in human nature itself; but what shall we say of the difficulties which lie outside of self, both in the temptations and the circumstances, which are often adverse, or seem adverse, to a high development? One discovers around him the very set of conditions which he would not have selected, and which appear calculated to produce just the opposite results from those which he desires. Imagine a nature so constituted that its condition seems to require a visible object of complete confidence and devotion; and either it finds itself alone, or, what is worse, in life-long companionship with an opposing character; a person with fixed tastes doomed to live a life that gives them no scope, or is forced into pursuits exactly opposed to them. There are, as all people know who have arrived at maturity, what may be mildly called unpleasant things, which invade one's being. It really comes to this—that we have to construct our views of life from a stand-point which takes into account all its struggles and its sorrows, for experience teaches that these things are so common and regular that they are incidental to our career, and any view of life which ignores them, or treats them as merely accidental, is a childish conception, and unreal. Hence, all these contingencies have to be added on to the other conditions described from the internal nature of the man himself. Then come the temptations of life. The facility with which sin can be pursued, the promptings of the opinion and influence of the world. Selfishness is more at hand than unselfishness. Invariably there is the immediate reason for the selfish act, where the ground of an unselfish one seems hidden. Now this is not a pessimist picture. It is true to life, but it shows how easy it is to "wander" without being what is commonly called a base person, easy too for him who is in heart good and noble.

It has been said that education teaches a man his ignorance. It appears equally true that religious culture teaches a man his weakness. When we learn the true value of knowledge we discover the feebleness of ignorance. So, too, when we study the ideal of moral excellence, we become impressed with our imperfection. In surveying the stature of a moral giant, we begin to estimate our humble figure. Now, this must be taken in its right sense. It must not disparage, it must not paralyse effort. In the struggle after righteousness there comes humility, but along with it its companion strength. Hence the soul need not be baffled. "When I said, My foot slippeth, Thy mercy, O Lord, held me up" (Psalm xciv. 18). This is the strength of the humble man. And, indeed, after each fall may he not rise stronger? For while an additional experience of sin must inevitably plunge the soul into deeper waters of humiliation, making it more dissatisfied with itself, there is surely in this very process a purification going on, and a refining, till sin gradually becomes less and less possible. If, on the other hand, the sense of having sinned had the effect of drowning the soul by making the effort of regeneration appear hopeless, there would be an end to moral progress. This evidently is not the design of religion, it cannot be the Divine Will. Here we may observe the difference between the Divine and the human judgment. When we see revenge in man there is compassion in God. Human condemnation appears where Divine pity is bestowed. Let it not be supposed that sin is justified, or that by any means we may pardon ourselves by making a wrong act right in our personal opinion. This is not meant by Divine mercy, nor is it in accordance with the strict justice which morality requires. The meaning of Divine mercy is not to shelter evil, but to deliver from evil, and so in our human speculations we have not to seek a refuge for sin, or even an excuse for it, but a way out of it, and this is true contrition; that there always is a way out of sin is a fact of infinite mercy. It must not be pretended that a wandering from righteousness can be condoned because contrition may come afterwards to bring back the wanderer. All we can contend is this: that the possibility of returning to God is never lost, though the terrors of falling away, however slightly, are still real, and, therefore, must be dreaded.

Against those terrors a pure soul will strive and labour. For some temperaments the strife is greater and the labour more laborious according to the measure of the temptation, and in proportion to the stability of character. But even where a character is considered stable and temptations seem far away, there may be one particular kind of error to which one is mysteriously subjected. Perhaps this is so with the best. There is some matter which jars on our inclination. There may be one single condition of life which, either from its absence or its presence, acts as a frequent hindrance, and in one detail it may occur that every now and then there comes an inward battle to be fought. Those who know much about human nature must perceive that in some beautiful lives there are clouds and discontent; there is turmoil which the eye of the world cannot see, and the source of which is hidden from all but the eye of

God and the poor lonely self who feels it, but who may perhaps not detect its source, and that poor lonely self is baffled and waylaid and wanders. It may arise from the disposition, sometimes from a state of health, a secret disappointment, a termination of a career, or a part of a career, which was not anticipated; occasionally there is the appalling hardship of being called upon suddenly to accommodate oneself to a new state of things for which there was no preparation. When we come into close contact with death it is necessary to shape our life anew, because up to the moment of the event the life was constituted, as it were, with the lost human object as a part of it. It happens sometimes that circumstances arise which place one fact of ordinary life and of natural desire quite beyond the state of possibility, and that poor self has to re-adjust itself to the altered things, the changed prospects.

All these contingencies are among the ills "which flesh is heir to," and they must be considered in any plan we lay down for a high moral culture. To wait till they arrive, or to consider that they are only problematical and may never occur, is to attempt to build up ethics and religion on a false basis. They are inevitable in the lives of good people, and no one is able to estimate the extraordinary variety in which they appear. The fact is, we know very little of each other, and the real secrets of life are known only to Him who sees in secret. It is this confidence in the Almighty God, which we gain from the conviction that only He knows all about us, that attracts the spirit to Him. Our consciousness of this perfect knowledge of us by God, together with the certainty that He is in Himself Absolute Righteousness, gives the hope to the words under consideration. In asking God to let us not wander from His commandments, especially in the same breath with the confession, "With my whole heart have I sought Thee," we are in reality taking the surest means against wandering, for we recognise in Him what it is that we fear wandering from, and we confess also the means by which we can be protected. To consider what that is from which we would not wander is to take a glimpse at the Divine Image, for it is His own Perfect Righteousness, the very thought of which fills the reverent mind with awe and worship. The worshipping of it is the lifting of ourselves, for a time at least, into fellowship with it. By its rules we hope to be governed. And what are those rules? The application in all cases of strict justice is one of them. The training of the will by its rigour, the consecration of every secret motive by the Divine love, which knows no selfishness, which bears all burdens; and the cleansing of every hidden thought by the purity of His Divine Omniscience. To take a course like this is a great effort. It is not easy to realise. It takes time, it uses circumstances, it avails itself of suffering, it employs sorrow. It is a course of rigour, but it is also a course of mercy. Its slow work with the possible, nay probable, many halts, gradually destroys pride and egotism; but as surely it prepares a sanctified soil for human tilling. Its fruits may be seen on this earth, and often are, but its end is not here. No! perhaps only its probation, for that word "end" is lost in Eternity!

"O LET ME NOT WANDER FROM THY COMMANDMENTS."

THE MASTER OF BALLIOL
(Professor Jowett).
In Memoriam.

[Reprinted from the " Jewish Chronicle," October 6th, 1893]

THOSE words which he took for the text of his sermon at Westminster Abbey the summer before last (1892) seem to drop out of one's pen in writing about the Master. "I have been young, and now am old; yet have I not seen the righteous forsaken" (Psalm xxxvii.). His excessive accuracy of thought probably prevented his quoting the entire verse. The sermon on that occasion was about John Wesley, that is to say, Wesley was the name he brought forward as the illustration of the virtues he was speaking upon, just as this year at his annual discourse in the Abbey he took for his examples John Bunyan and Spinoza. But the real subject of the sermon in 1892 was the experience in old age that the righteous are never really forsaken. Righteousness, and indeed the mere contemplation of goodness, were most powerful ideals in Jowett's character. Anyone who has read his introduction to the *Republic* will perceive that the Master of Balliol was a man of ideals. This is not always understood in regard to him because he was very practical. And the ideal which was most prominent was the ideal of goodness. It seems almost a paradox to say of a man who is pre-eminently identified with great intellectual achievement that he was above all things a man of goodness. Yes! that he was in the real homely tender sense a person to whom the claims of righteousness came first. It is quite certain that among the numerous people, including scholars and statesmen, who revere him, the people who loved him most were just those who, it might be supposed, were separated from him by immeasureable gulfs, belonging to an intellectual level so far beneath his own. Such persons, including his servants, did not care about him on account of his having produced in perfect English the thoughts and works of Plato, Thucydides, and Aristotle; nor because of the wonderful part he has taken in the reconstruction of the religious beliefs of educated men; they were devoted to him through the attraction which his singular goodness had for them. They found him so just, so exceptionally unselfish. He awakened in all kinds of different people a truly filial sense of devotion. Jowett was great by reason of the simplicity of his character, quite independently of the other reason of his greatness. It is not every genius who can make himself loved. Before these words are in print, memoirs without number will have appeared. But there yet remain the individual tributes of different persons to whom he was inexpressibly dear. And each will speak and write as he found him.

When I first knew the Master he was physically in the zenith of his vigour. He was about 59 years of age, and was probably the most active head of a college—certainly without precedent either at Oxford or Cambridge. Adorned with the maturity of advanced life, he had not yet any of the physical infirmities of old age. Up to the last he had none of the ordinary infirmities of age, except physical ones. Intellectually there was no perceptible or real difference this year from the year 1876. At that time he was one of the hardest worked men in England. He was in the midst of his translation of Thucydides, and he was at the same time delivering his lectures on the Politics of Aristotle. He knew every undergraduate in Balliol more or less. Every Saturday morning he presided before 9 a.m. in the College hall at the function of distributing the weekly accounts called "Battells" to each undergraduate. The Master always cast his eye over each paper, and invariably commented to any individual who he considered was either living beyond his means or indulging in extravagance. So minute was his supervision over the details of the College life that once a week it was the duty of the Dinner Committee to have an interview with him on the subject of the dinner arrangements. There were two undergraduates elected by the College from term to term for this purpose. I happened to occupy the post one year with a colleague, who sometimes made me go alone to this weekly conference. The reports concerning the dinners in the Hall generally seemed so trivial that one hesitated to tell the Master anything about them, but he always insisted upon knowing and sometimes would remark, "Life is made up of little things, and men's capacity for work is hindered if the potatoes are not properly cooked." Although these interviews were intensely comic from the undergraduate's point of view, and engendered a special shyness which seemed to be created for the occasion, the Master went about the business in quite a serious tone, and would send for the butler or the housekeeper afterwards if necessary. In those days the Master would allow an undergraduate to consult him about such matters as the situation of his rooms and similar domestic details. Nothing which affected the conditions of work, whether they were intellectual or merely physical, appeared indifferent to him.

It is needless to say that religious equality was one of the ideals of his life, and that he was the first "don" of Oxford who made religious intolerance there an impossibility. For two or three terms I was the only Jew in Balliol, though I found two others there when I first went up. They were both people to whom in different ways the Master was personally attached. One was

Solomon, who had the University Mathematical Scholarship, and possessed striking classical attainments; the other was the ever-lamented Leonard Montefiore, one of the most brilliant men in or out of Balliol. His brother, Claude, came up in my second year. Gradually other members of the Jewish community appeared at Balliol; the more notable that I remember (in my third year) were Kalisch, Sidney Lee (the present Editor of the Dictionary of National Biography), and Alexander, Fellow of Lincoln. There have been a host of others since that time, including sons of the late Professor Waley, the late Sir George Jessel, and of Mr. Arthur Cohen, Q.C. The Master, who was of all men singularly exempt from prejudice of every species, had a preference for those Jews who were staunch to their faith, and rather regarded with contempt the renegade type. He was most desirous that we should organise religious worship for Jews at Oxford, and revive the dilapidated congregation of that ancient city. It was largely owing to his encouragement that one or two of us ventured to undertake this in the year 1878. We succeeded for our time, then our efforts lapsed in their results; and it has been reserved for a later generation of undergraduates to succeed with something like permanent effect in the last two years.

Professor Jowett signed the two requisitions to the Lord Mayor on the persecution of the Jews in Russia — both in 1882 and 1890. On the former occasion he wrote these words, which were read at the Mansion House Meeting: "The cruelties which have been inflicted on the Jews in Russia, as narrated by the correspondent of the *Times*, are detestable, and should be denounced by the unanimous opinion of civilised nations." He, of course, signed the Oxford requisition from resident dons and Masters of Arts addressed to the Chief Rabbi at that time. These are, however, matters which in relation to Jowett are of the merest detail. What he has done for the cause of religion, for the emancipation of the higher life from the thraldom of dogmatism, is the subject in which modern Judaism, or the religion of modern Jews, is profoundly concerned. Biblical criticism is a modern science, of which Professor Jowett may be said to have started investigation at Oxford in the year 1861 by the publication of his memorable essay on the "Interpretation of Scripture." Two years earlier the appearance of his "Notes and Dissertations," on the chief Epistles of St. Paul, indicated a great movement towards a rational understanding of vital questions in the Christian Bible. The Master was not eager in later life to revive the controversies which that work had evoked. He did not love controversy, and would regard with a kindly and yet piteous scorn those contentions in which many orthodox Christians rejoiced. The religion of Jowett was in some respects widely different from that of ordinary Christians. Only the year before last he denounced in Westminster Abbey the pernicious doctrine of eternal punishment, not indeed for the first time. He did not believe that a particular creed was necessary to salvation. In other words Jowett may be regarded as the apostle of the doctrine of development in religion. People of different epochs and of changed standards of intellectual training cannot regard even an inherited faith from quite the same stand-point. He was indeed a Reformer of Reformers, and viewed the religious life as something wholly independent of the conditions from which it was once thought to be inseparable. The characteristic of Jowett's sermons, which marked them off from all other sermons, was just the absence of everything and anything which could seem to label them. They were not High Church, Low Church, or Agnostic. They were full of piety, overflowing with wisdom, and were usually applicable as much to the followers of one creed as to those of another. Often they might as well have been spoken in a synagogue as in a church or a chapel. He spoke about virtue, and about God, but never about an "Article." We have heard him preach on Friendship, on Sympathy, on the Love of God, but not upon the "Incarnation" or the "Resurrection." He illustrated his points by reference to Christian saints, to Jewish sages, and to Greek philosophers. But he did not seem to consider that we could learn only from the one—not from the other. Perhaps it will be remarked hereafter that Jowett believed in the unity of religion. Religion with him was a great force in human character—not the representation of a sect or a church. Nine sermons out of ten were prefixed with this collect: "O Lord, Who hast taught us that all our doings without charity are nothing worth," and the tenth would be preceded by the well-known prayer: "Prevent us, O God, in all our doings, by Thy most gracious favour, and further us with Thy continual help, that in all our works, begun, continued and ended in Thee, we may worthily magnify Thy holy name and finally by Thy mercy obtain everlasting life." These were his two leading ideas in religion—human charity and faith in the guiding power of God. Yet there are those who would regard Jowett as an unbeliever and a destroyer of faith. He was with few exceptions the most religious man it was possible to know. And those who knew him best, when listening to his exhortations, could recall incidents in his own life in which he proved that his high standard of goodness and of purity was not unattainable. In respect to soundness of judgment upon the ordinary, or even the exceptional affairs of life, he was the safest counsellor. He possessed the most wonderful imagination. He could always understand a situation in a moment. No person ever had a deeper insight into the characters of others or a wider knowledge of human nature. His capacity for forming and for maintaining friendships was quite extraordinary. It is probably correct to say that there is no man in England who had so many friends, or who was the friend, I mean the true and trusted confidant, of so many persons. True as steel, one could always rely upon him that he would give the best possible advice. He seemed to possess a boundless human sympathy, and whether the question to be decided was the choice of a profession, the course of study, or the management of worldly affairs, the Master was the person of all others whom it was desirable to consult. His kindness of heart was truly remarkable. He would often write a letter to an undergraduate, who was ill, and advise him what to read by way of recreation. Like all truly interesting characters he was endowed with a keen sense of humour. He used to make a practice of offering rewards to young men who could tell the best story at a breakfast, or make the best original joke. In the afternoon walks he would always give a light turn to the conversation because he thought that during physical exercise the mind ought not to be exerted too much. He was very generous about people's defects of character unless they happened to be vanity and conceit. Those were failings that he could not brook. If he was dealing with an egotistical individual in middle life he would pour upon him the most scathing criticism or the bitterest sarcasm. If the offender were a younger person and an undergraduate he would simply observe, "You are a very conceited young man—do not be so foolish." Idleness was another vice to which he was not at all lenient. When he encountered these evils his speech was very direct and explicit. The effect of his words was almost mystical in their working upon the undergraduate's conscience. It is tolerably sure that many a man now in the prime of life owes the eradication of some such fault as those above named to the electrical words he heard from the Master. He was often severe but never hard. He could use satire when occasion justified it, but he was not a cynic. He took pains with men to bring out what was best in them. To those who were away from him, and rarely saw him for many years, the thought of his regard for them was like resting on a rock. He was there, ever ready and willing to be consulted, always able to help in some extraordinary way in which no other could be of service. And now it is only a memory—all that strength, all that moral courage, that great intellectual force, that remarkable personality, vanished into another world. Those of us who are familiar with the experience of the valley of the shadow of death see in this change a revelation of a life beyond the grave. Such a mind, such a character, such a spirit, cannot be perishable. And the thought of him as transferred to another life recalls his own dear words in that incomparable essay on the Immortality of the Soul: "First of all there is the thought of rest and freedom from pain; they have gone home, as the common saying is, and the cares of this world touch them no more. Secondly, we may imagine them as they were at their best and brightest, humbly fulfilling their daily round of duties—selfless, childlike, unaffected by the world; when the eye was single and the whole body seemed to be full of light; when the mind was clear and saw into the purposes of God. Thirdly, we may think of them as possessed by a great love of God and man, working out His will at a further stage in the heavenly pilgrimage." And to-day his body will be laid to rest in the soil of his beloved Oxford, surrounded by no kinsmen, but amid the affectionate tribute of a host of loving disciples.

www.ingramcontent.com/pod-product-compliance
Lightning Source LLC
Chambersburg PA
CBHW032108220426
43664CB00008B/1175